AF328048

THE LENORE AND BURTON GOLD
COLLECTION OF 20TH-CENTURY ART

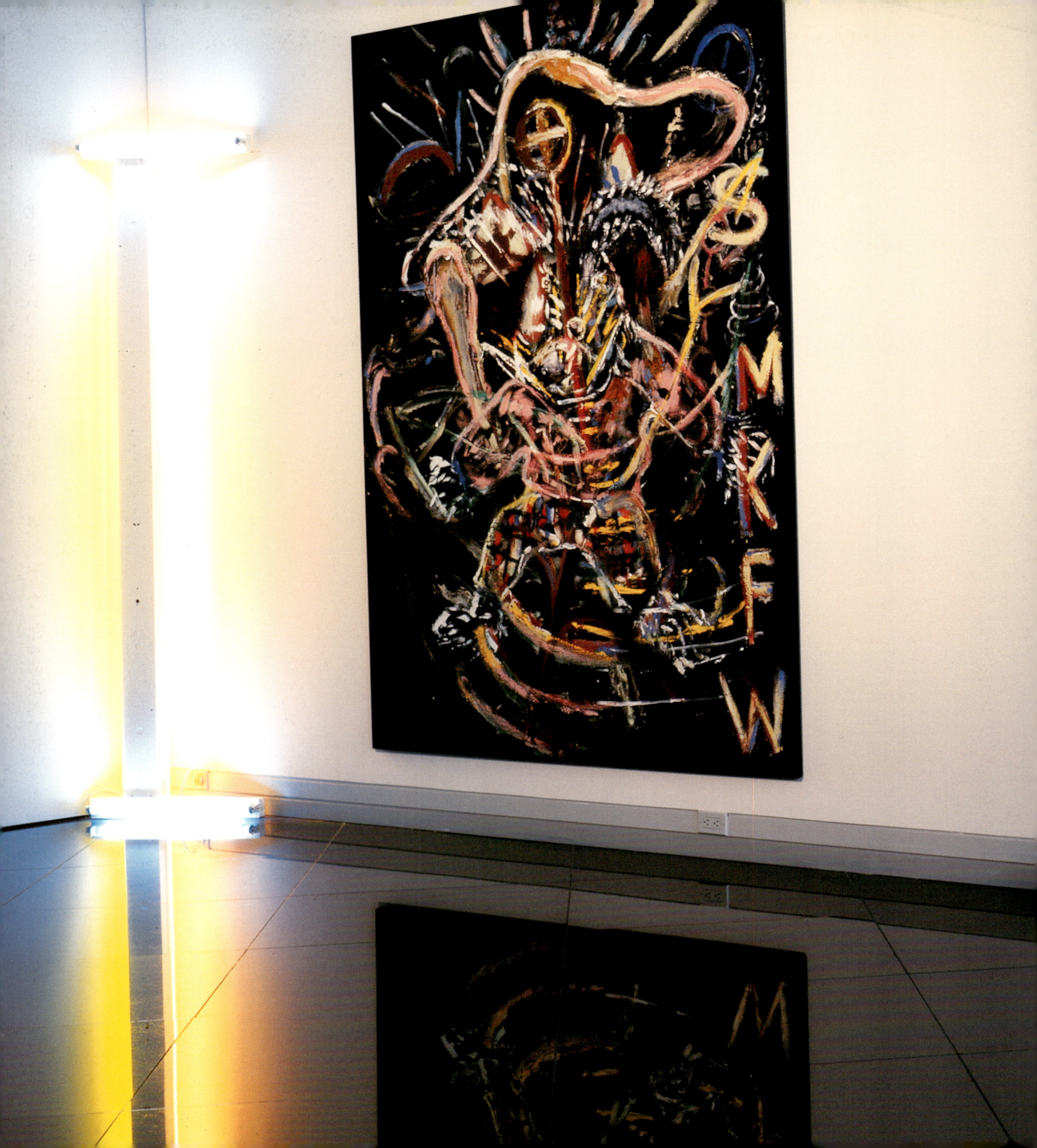

M
K
F
W

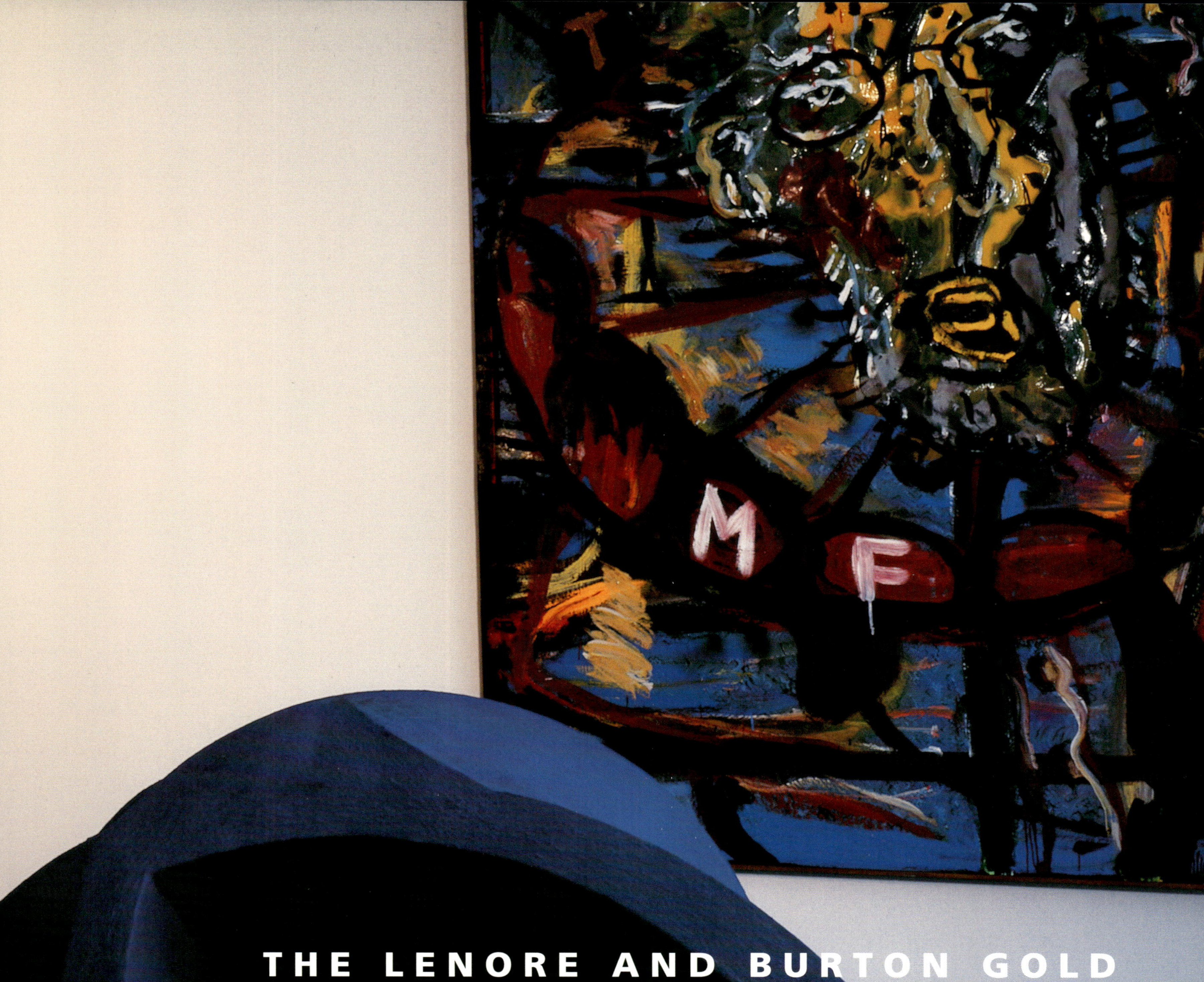

THE LENORE AND BURTON GOLD
COLLECTION OF 20TH-CENTURY ART

CARRIE PRZYBILLA, *curator*
Introduction by **PETER MORRIN**

High Museum of Art
ATLANTA

The Lenore and Burton Gold Collection of 20th-Century Art is organized by the High Museum of Art.

The Lenore and Burton Gold Collection of 20th-Century Art was on view at the High Museum of Art, Atlanta, from March 3 to May 27, 2001.

Unless otherwise noted (page 112), all photographs taken by Peter Harholdt.

ISBN: 0-939802-93-7
Library of Congress Control Number: 00-136447

Jacket front: Living room, Park Place, ca. 1995
Pages 2–3: Gallery, Park Place, ca. 1995

For the High Museum of Art
Kelly Morris, Manager of Publications
Nora E. Poling, Associate Editor
Janet S. Rauscher, Assistant Editor

Designed by Susan E. Kelly
Proofread by Sharon Rose Vonasch
Produced by Marquand Books, Inc., Seattle
  www.marquand.com
Printed by CS Graphics Pte., Ltd., Singapore

CONTENTS

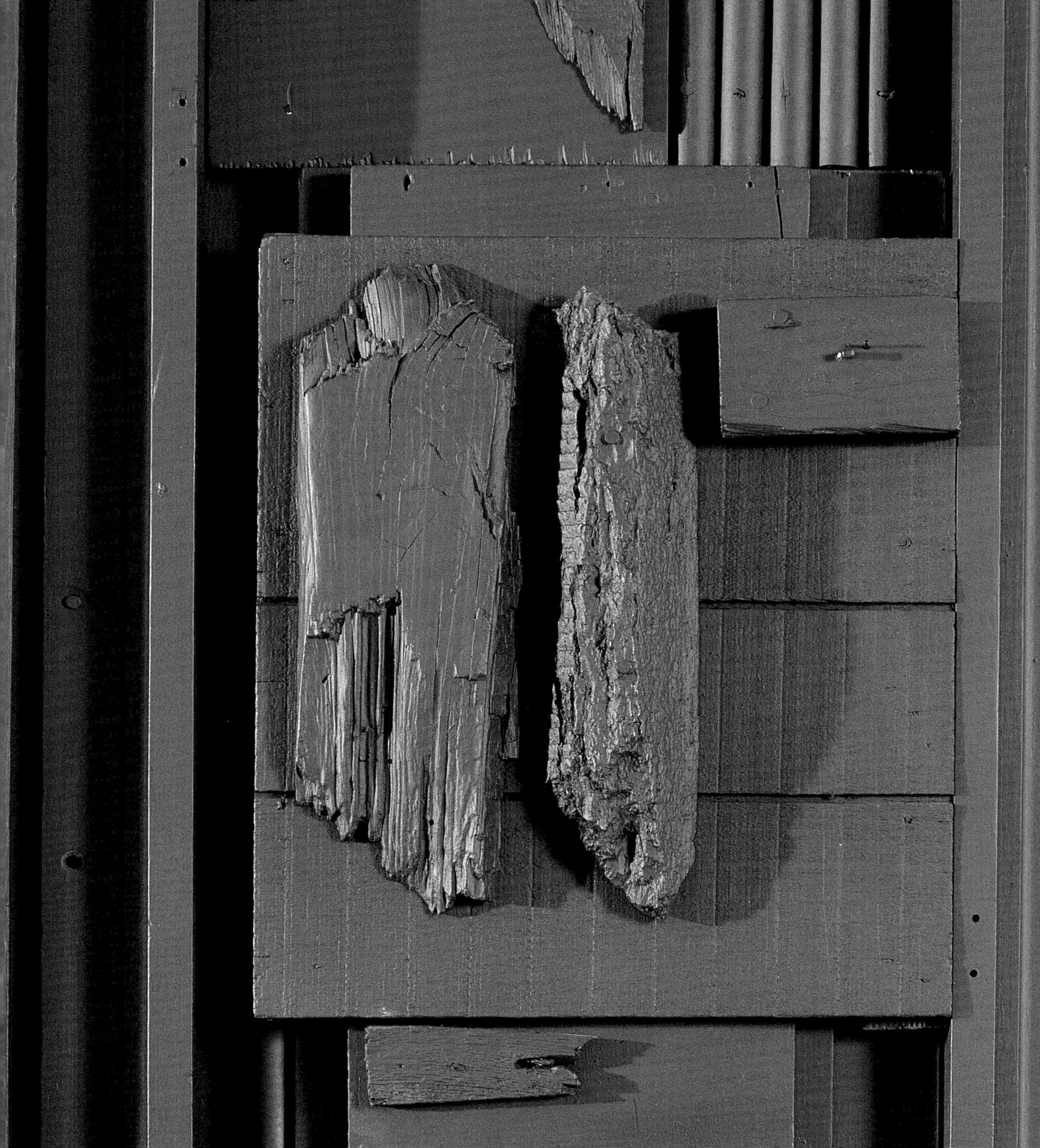

This catalogue accompanies an exhibition of works from the collection of Lenore and Burton Gold, and it celebrates a dynamic partnership. Lenore possessed an irrepressible spirit and a passion for the art of our time and worked tirelessly to promote the collecting of contemporary art in Atlanta. The exhibition and catalogue also pay tribute to Burt's appreciation of art, his steadfast support of Lenore's keen eye, and his wish to honor her memory. The gift to the High of the Lenore and Burton Gold Collection of 20th-Century Art represents the logical culmination of their devotion to each other, to art, and to the High Museum of Art.

We are deeply grateful to Burt for his generosity. The twenty-eight works he has given or promised to the High are significant additions to our holdings. In addition to thanking him, I wish to express my gratitude for the enthusiasm and assistance of his and Lenore's four daughters: Joanne Gold, Lauren G. Grien, Janice Gold Dietz, and Pamela Gold Alexander. Each has lent works she inherited to the exhibition and has taken an active role in perpetuating Leni's legacy. The gracious support of Barbara Gold has also been deeply appreciated.

Because this gift and exhibition resulted from the Golds' long relationship with the High, I am pleased to share credit with my predecessors, Gudmund Vigtel, Director Emeritus, and Ned Rifkin, Director of the Menil Foundation and Collection, for nurturing a strong relationship with the Golds. Peter Morrin, former Curator of 20th Century Art at the High and now Director of the J. B. Speed Art Museum in Louisville, Kentucky, has provided an introductory essay for this catalogue that beautifully describes the Golds' early collecting activities. I am grateful to him and to his successors, Susan Krane, now Director of the Colorado University Art Galleries, and Carrie Przybilla, the High's current Curator of Modern and Contemporary Art, for their efforts. In addition to her instrumental role in arranging the gift of the collection to the High, Carrie curated the exhibition and contributed texts for half the entries in this catalogue. I commend her for a job well done.

Several gifted writers have also lent their talents in providing entries for this catalogue: Amalia Amaki, Assistant Professor of Art History at Spelman College; Anna Bloomfield, former Associate Editor in the High's Publications Department; Trinkett Clark, an independent curator; Emily G. Hanna, Professor of Art History at Georgia State University; and Thomas W. Southall, the High's Curator of Photography. Their expertise and contributions have been invaluable to the production of this catalogue.

Of course, exhibitions such as this are always a team effort. For their good work in bringing this exhibition to fruition, I particularly wish to acknowledge Rhonda Matheison, Director of Finance and Operations; Sheldon Wolf, Director of Museum Advancement; Marjorie Harvey, Acting Director of Museum Programs; Frances Francis, Registrar; Laurie Hicks, Exhibition Coordinator; Melissa Thurmond, Senior Publicist; H. Nichols B. Clark, Eleanor McDonald Storza Chair of Education; Jim Waters, Chief Preparator; and Kelly Morris, Manager of Publications. The High is indeed fortunate to have such talented individuals on our staff.

Michael E. Shapiro
Nancy and Holcombe T. Green, Jr. Director

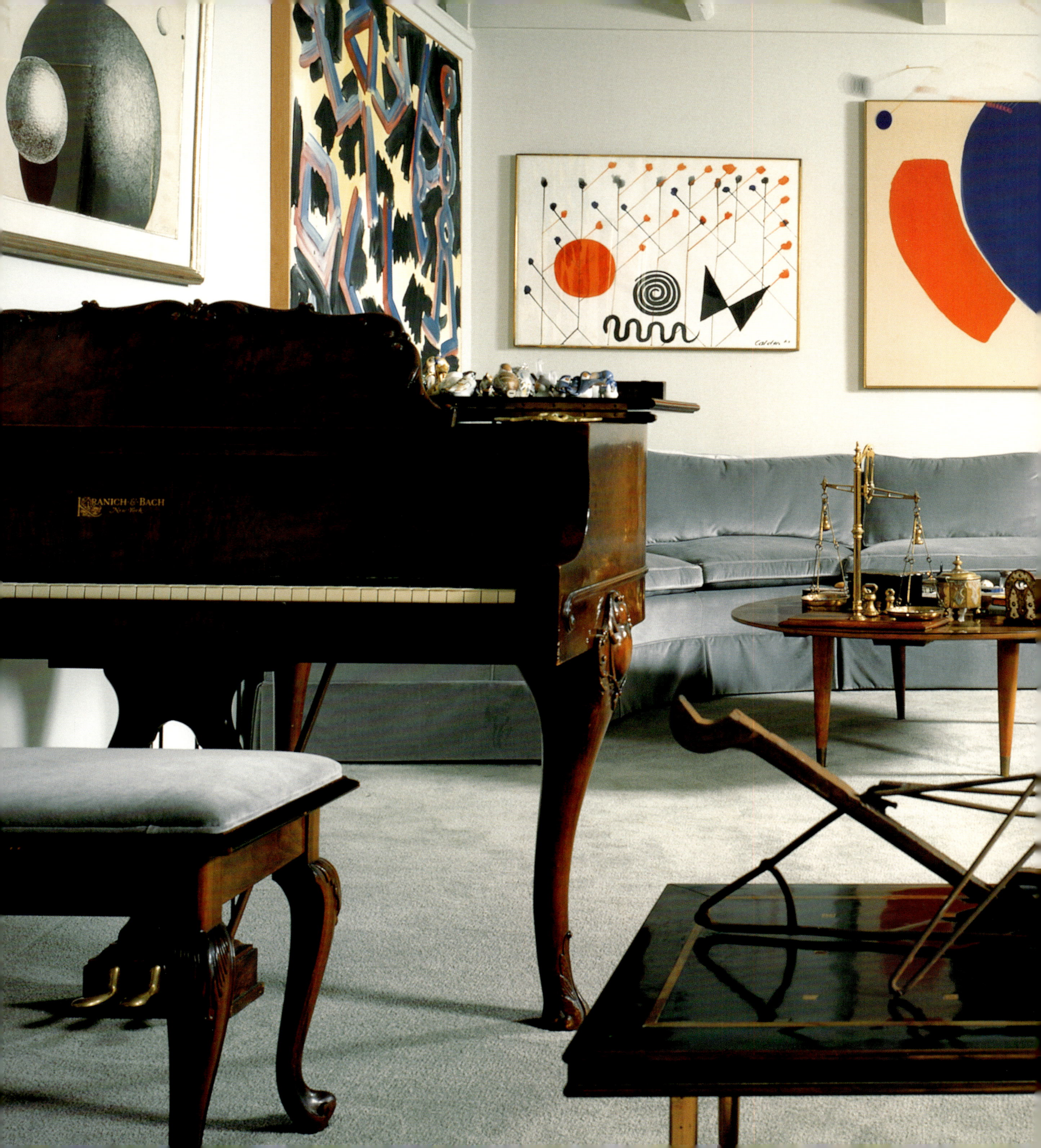

THE REVOLUTION ON REMBRANDT ROAD

Peter Morrin

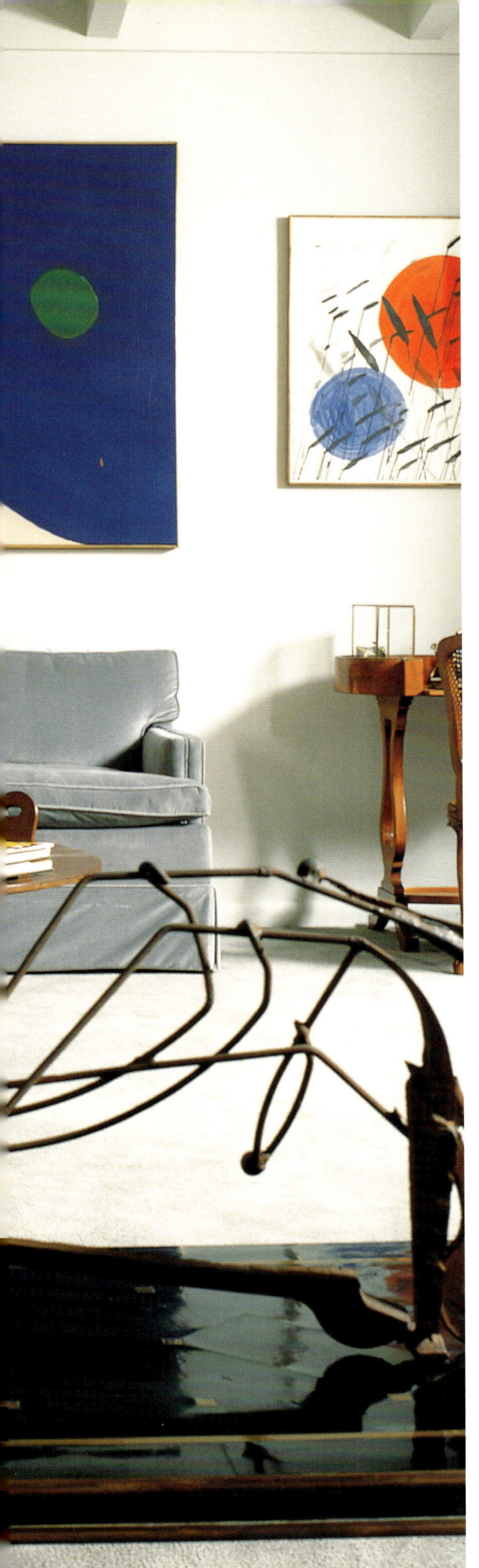

In 1979 traffic in midtown Atlanta was mod-erate. Taylor's Drugstore, one block from the High Museum of Art on Peachtree Street, sold a fried pork chop sandwich for $1.75. Charlie Yates, president of the Atlanta Arts Alliance, often had his favorite lunch there: a bowl of vegetable soup with a side order of greens added in, topped by crumbled corn bread. Only seven years later, traffic had metastasized, a high-rise office building had replaced Taylor's, and Atlanta boasted a range of cuisine appropriate for "the world's next great city." In those years Atlanta's visual sophistication also made enormous strides, and at the heart of this evolution was collector and patron Lenore Gold.

The High Museum was then within the Memorial Arts Center building in a warren of spaces that felt more like a down-market department store than an art museum. Late in that year Eric Zafran and I came to take positions as Curator of European Art and Curator of 20th Century Art, respectively. Donald Peirce in Decorative Arts arrived a few months later. Curators were new and exotic in Atlanta then, and it seemed that a great many people wanted a look at us. In an apogee of Southern hospitality, we were paraded before the public in a grand round of brunches, luncheons, teas, cocktail parties, dinners, and late-night suppers. Most of our hosts were on the Museum Board, but (as I was soon to learn) few were actively engaged in looking at and acquiring very recent art.

The three curators began to share the burdens that Director Gudmund Vigtel had manfully shouldered alone for nearly two decades. The High itself had acquired well in contemporary art, albeit not in great quantities. Mrs. Frances Floyd Cocke, whose heart was really in the Dr. Wall period of Worcester porcelain, was very generous: following Vigtel's guidance, a great Frank Stella protractor variation, *Manteneia I,* was her gift as well as works by Kenneth Noland and Elizabeth Murray.

John Howett and Clark Poling, professors at Emory University, were active at the High as guest curators, lecturers, and warm supporters of Vigtel's efforts on behalf of contemporary art. John Howett's show of Martin Emanuel's sublimely numinous light sculptures was a highlight of my first year in Atlanta; equally provocative was Clark Poling's comprehensive survey of Los Angeles art. Both Ed Moses and Robert Irwin did site-specific installations for that show. But there were no acquisitions from these terrific exhibitions.

At this time, art and collecting circles in Atlanta spun in distantly tangential orbits. Bob Fusillo, whose primary interest was in European artists such as Richard Smith, Horst Antes, Barbara Hepworth, and Henry Moore, represented one pole. Collectors Mark and Judith Taylor shared many of Bob's interests. Photography enthusiasts rallied around the collector-photographer-writer team of Lucinda Bunnen and Virginia Warren Smith: Jay Crouse's Atlanta Gallery of Photography was one of their haunts. At one remove was Nexus, then primarily a photography venue. Leading Atlanta photographers like Jim Frazer, John McWilliams, and Chip Simone showed there.

Yet another group of collectors and artists were centered around the David Heath Gallery, where Southern artists like New Orleans painter Ida Kohlmeyer and Atlanta minimalists Katherine Mitchell, Ed Ross, Annette Cone-Skelton, and Genevieve Arnold could be seen, along with a stunning selection of Jasper Johns and Robert Rauschenberg prints from U.L.A.E. David Heath had several shows from the stable of artists represented by Paula Cooper Gallery in New York, notably Carl Andre, Lynda Benglis, and Alan Shields.

Living room, Rembrandt Road, 1984

Following their own muse were collectors like the Regensteins, Levins, Seligs, Elsons, and James H. Grady, who had little interaction with Atlanta's galleries or its nascent collecting circles. Collecting in Atlanta was then a solitary and eccentric pursuit.

Finally, there was Judith Alexander, who had the best eye of all and who introduced the work of Southern self-taught artists in her gallery, especially Nellie Mae Rowe. With her encouragement, a group of artists, including Susan Loftin, Don Cooper, Amy Landesberg, and Beth Bolga, developed a self-consciously Southern style, with cognates in Athens, Georgia, in the work of Andy Nasisse and Art Rosenberg.

The Atlanta Arts Festival in Piedmont Park undergirded these activities, and *Art Papers* documented them.

In this disjunctive maelstrom, Lenore Gold became a unifier, an educator, an organizer, and a driving force. And she gave the High primacy of place in her efforts.

Dialogue with Leni began shortly after my arrival. After the first flurry of hospitality, the dinner parties continued, and more and more of them were at the Golds. The guest lists were smaller and the dinner companions more active as collectors. The guests were typically not lifelong Atlantans but relatively new arrivals to the South and not well represented in the High's inner circles. Nonetheless, Leni already had a following in 1979. She had been chair of the Arts Festival of Atlanta, and she organized and led trips to New York to visit galleries. Soon Leni had me lecturing to her groups. Other speaking engagements followed with her connivance, such as the Brandeis University National Women's Committee, where for years she led art study groups. Leni was an intuitive expert in the care and feeding of museum curators, and she knew that they needed frequent exposure to a variety of audiences. Indeed, her intuition was almost telepathic, and her understanding of people and their problems, her willingness to get involved and help solve those problems, made life more enjoyable in general for those around her. She saw herself as a catalyst for positive change, and she was.

The Gold home on Rembrandt Road was a long narrow ranch. Visits in the morning began with a cup of coffee at the breakfast table, a Susan Loftin ceramic house the centerpiece. In the afternoon, the living room was the setting, opera playing in the background. Brie, a black toy poodle who viewed me with deep suspicion, barked furiously until Leni picked her up. The furniture was traditional, and the coffee table was covered with a large collection of snuffboxes.

Leni gained the warm support of her husband Burton early in her collecting days. While still living in New York in about 1967, she purchased a Joan Miró lithograph from a very small edition for $450. She was quite pleased with its rapid appreciation in value within approximately six months of acquiring the piece and conveyed this to Burt. He, as a businessman and not yet in tune with her love for the art, said, "If you can do so well in such a short period of time, you ought to sell the work and buy something else." Tearfully, one Saturday morning she removed the piece from the wall and drove with him from their home in New Rochelle, New York, to Manhattan. Burt dropped her off on Madison Avenue at a gallery she had selected and then proceeded to his office. About an hour later, Burt recalls that he received a call from Leni saying, "Let's meet for lunch. And bring a check for $300." "What's that for?" he asked. She answered, "I doubled my money on the Miró and found another piece I want to buy. It costs $1,200." From then on, Burt always deferred to her judgement about art. Although she selected and purchased works that she liked, she made sure that he could also be happy with them.

The core of the Gold collection in 1979 was the work of Alexander Calder. There was a large group of Calder gouaches (see cat. 4), showing all aspects of his surreal imagination, as well as a mobile (cat. 5). Complementing these works were several important early Miró etchings and a Miró drawing (see cats. 26–27), some African art (see cat. 28), and a selection of photographs by Arnold Newman, Lee Friedlander, and others. Other artists in favor were Alex Katz (see cat. 16) and Philip Pearlstein, both represented by works on paper. A small painted wood construction by Betty Parsons (cat. 34) was bright and colorful, while a large gray Olitski painting (cat. 32) provided a more subtle example of Leni's taste for color. A George Segal wood and plaster construction of a girl partially seen behind a door (cat. 37) and a tall Nevelson box (cat. 29) were standouts.

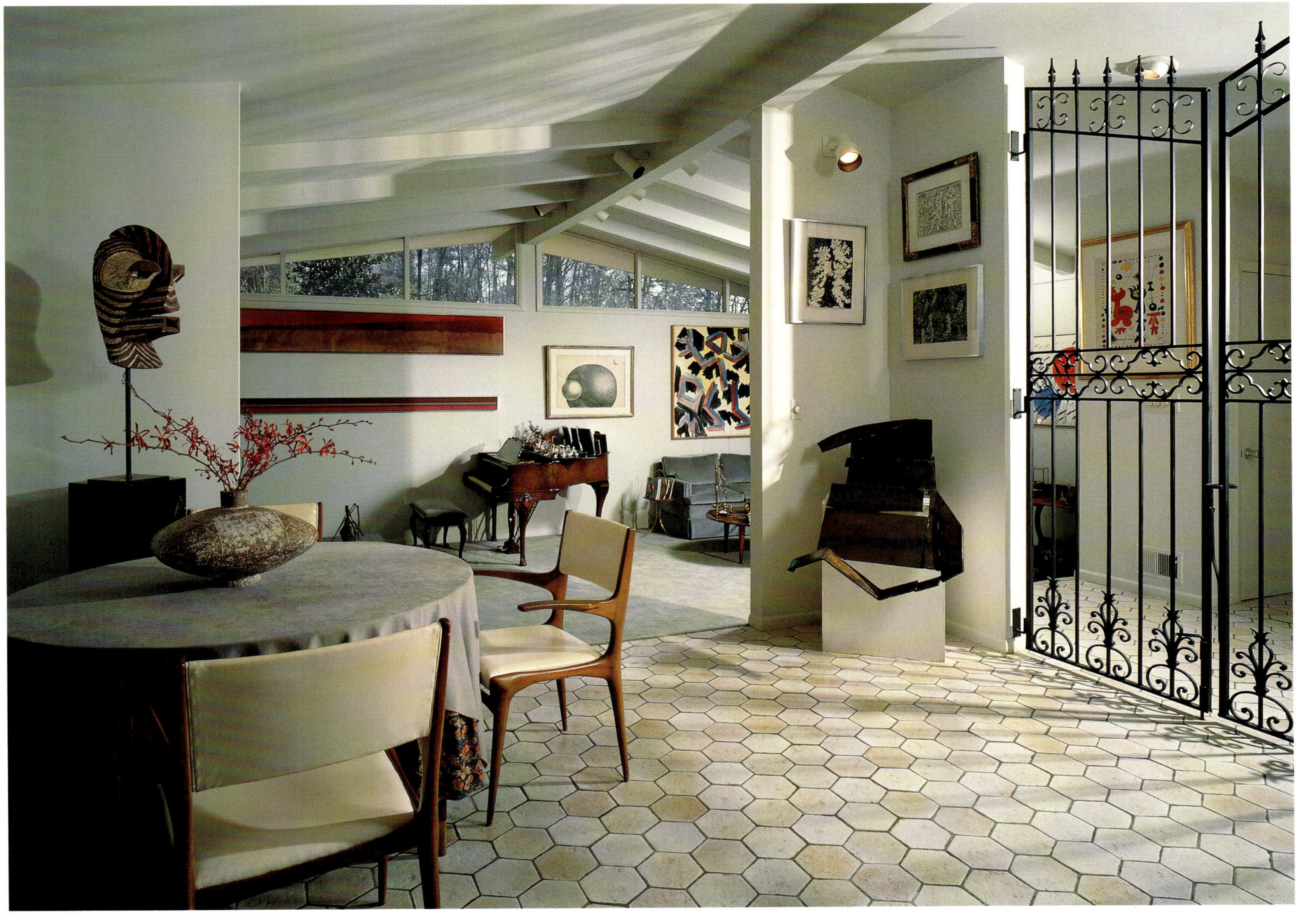

Dining room, Rembrandt Road, 1984

A special love of three-dimensional works was apparent on Rembrandt Road.

The collection in 1979 was contemporary but safe: representational art and the joyous Calders struck the major chords. Everything could be easily appreciated. The collection reflected Leni's comfort zone, but it also reflected her personality: the Calders and Mirós were a natural backdrop for such a warm and exuberant person, and the representational works were a reflection of her concern and sentiment for others. From the start she tended to be loyal to artists, either buying more than one work or selling and buying up to get a better example.

Leni soon became someone with whom to confer about ideas for exhibitions. In quick succession, I did small shows of Rauschenberg and Johns graphics and Jennifer Bartlett's drawings for her Russell Courthouse commission, *Swimmers Atlanta.* Leni steered me to the collectors with the right pieces to borrow or schemed to get people to buy works so that the art would stay in town. She was a great help when Eric Zafran and I organized a show in 1981 of nineteenth- and twentieth-century drawings in Georgia collections. The exhibition was the beginning of a realization that there were ambitious collectors in the region who needed to be drawn more closely

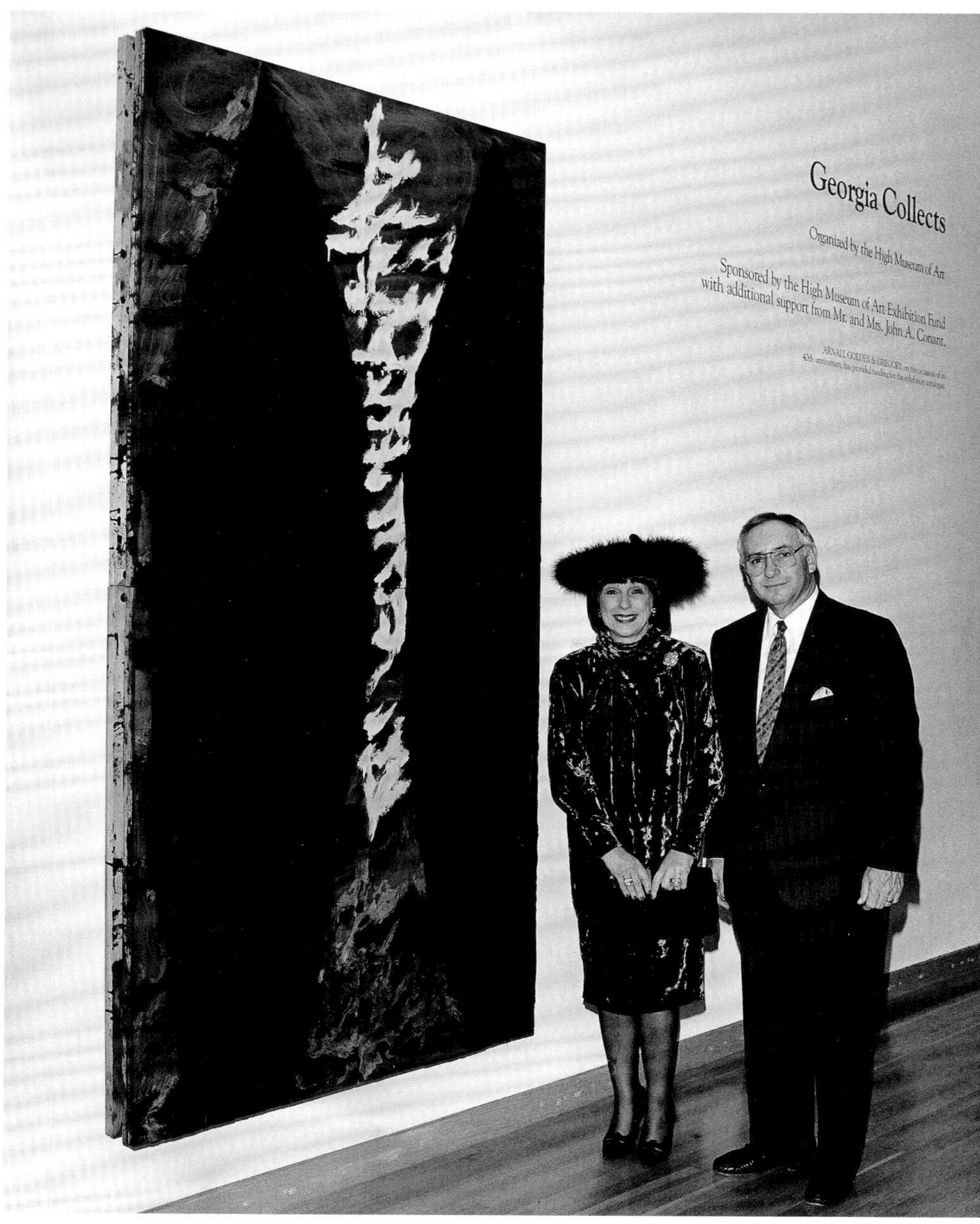

Lenore and Burton Gold with Donald Sultan's *Forest Fire, March 20, 1984* (cat. 42) at the opening of the exhibition *Georgia Collects* at the High Museum of Art, 24 January–26 March 1989.

into the Museum's circle. Gudmund Vigtel wrote in the preface to that exhibition, "Quite often, works held by private individuals play an important part in a community's cultural growth, though the art may not be on public view."[1] Shortly, this was to be the role played by the Golds' collection.

The spring of 1981 also saw the formation of the 20th Century Art Society of the High Museum of Art. While Leni was not the first chairman (she succeeded Genevieve Arnold and Mark Taylor, who were the first co-chairs), she was certainly a prime motivator. The goals of the organization were to educate Atlantans about art in general and modern art in particular; to provide opportunities to share interest in twentieth-century art; and to provide a means of generating support for twentieth-century art at the High. Lectures, visits to Atlanta collections and artists' studios, and trips to New York and the Chicago Art Fair were the group's offerings. The first board of the 20th Century Art Society was very diverse, brought together as much by Leni's persuasion and cajoling as by common interests. Mark Taylor, the only parliamentarian in the group, struggled mightily to keep a tenuous grasp on the agenda. The important exchanges happened before and after the meeting: Dr. Stan Cohen showing drawings on veneer by a young artist named Carroll Dunham, Medford Johnson announcing a visit from Chicago dealers Donald Young and Rhona Hoffman, or Bob Fusillo, just back from a sabbatical in England, exulting about young British sculptors Tony Cragg, Anish Kapoor, and Bill Woodrow.

Collecting in a sense became a team sport. Leni's vast handbag was the repository of transparencies, which she showed me in my office, at her house, at openings, lectures, and dinner parties . . . anywhere. The dream of every contemporary art curator is to foster competition among a museum's loyal friends for the newest, most challenging work from New York, Paris, Los Angeles, or Berlin. In an oddly collaborative way, that is what happened. No board meeting of the 20th Century Art Society began without transparencies from Leni's purse being passed around.

While the evolution was rapid, it occurred with a few bumps and rough spots. With an overweening concern for my curatorial prerogatives, I told Leni that I thought her tours to New York conflicted with my potential Museum excursions.

She was not only a teacher and mentor for her collectors, but she also sold graphics to her travel companions. She acquiesced, and her role at the Museum grew. She and Burt began to be more regular donors to the High: Eric Zafran and I admired a particularly joyous and erotic Walkowitz drawing from his long series of depictions of Isadora Duncan (cat. 44), and it came straight off the Golds' dining room wall as a gift to the High Museum.

Photography was a major Museum preoccupation in the early 1980s, and the Golds obliged in 1982 with Garry Winogrand's *Coney Island, New York* (cat. 45). Another gift was a lithograph by Alex Katz of a woman in the rain (cat. 16): the print was no longer something the Golds needed to live with, and this gift indicated the beginning of a shift in taste away from more conventional images. While not major works in themselves, these gifts were signals of good faith and commitment to the Museum.

The founding of the 20th Century Art Society also coincided with Atlanta's emergence from a recession. Real estate development and other opportunities brought commissions in the early to mid-1980s for David Saunders, Louise Nevelson, George Trakas, Robert Therrien, Anthony Gormley, and Jackie Winsor.[2] Jeff Kipnis opened an art gallery that showed paintings by Leon Golub and architectural drawings. Jane Bickerton held exhibitions in her home of prints by Sandro Chia, Enzo Cucchi, Francesco Clemente, Richard Smith, Howard Hodgkins, and Yvonne Rainer, among many others. In the early 1980s the Arts Festival of Atlanta commissioned site-specific works from Carl Andre, Cecile Abish, Robert Morris, Houston Conwill, and Scott Burton. Visiting speakers included critics Klaus Kertess and A. D. Coleman, print publisher Kathan Brown, and artists William Wegman, Sam Gilliam, Joel Shapiro, John Coplans, Joan Snyder, Chuck Close, and David Hammons. The availability of information and events regarding contemporary art mushroomed. The opening of Richard Meier's new building in the fall of 1983 provided the greatest stimulus of all: suddenly collectors of new art could envision a place on the walls of the High for gifts from their collections in a setting far more complementary than the old halls next door.

This activity stimulated Leni's collecting, although she remained highly independent in her

taste. The pace began to accelerate with the purchase of works by Anthony Caro and Jules Olitski (cat. 31). I responded with a small lobby show of Caros in Atlanta collections. A Kenneth Noland painting followed—the High bought a fine Noland subsequently (again the angel was Fanny Cocke), and Mark and Judith Taylor bought a Noland as well. Communal connoisseurship began to emerge.

At the beginning of the 1980s, Leni's taste was stirred by the formalist construct of a decade earlier. The Caro—soon to be accompanied by another work by the artist—was from the artist's series called "Writing Sculptures," small informal works whose graceful, offhand qualities struck a chord with the Calders and the Miró. The Olitski, the second one in the collection (cat. 31), was a 1963 color field painting with deeply saturated greens and blues. The exchange among Atlantans included an interchange of dealers' names, and a favorite at that time was Stewart Waltzer, who had been Kenneth Noland's studio assistant. Waltzer had wonderful color field paintings to show from his Bowery loft. With Olitski, Leni recognized the market opportunity but also worked her way around to an early work of a phase of Olitski's career that was not particularly celebrated. The purchase demonstrated Leni's independence of mind and willingness to pursue an atypical work of art. The Noland, no less idiosyncratic, was a very beautiful, very narrow stripe painting that hung high on the living room wall, not far below the ceiling. As a collector, Leni favored artists slightly out of fashion who were solidly established: it was orthodox Museum of Modern Art taste with an emphasis on formal values.

In 1984, a small group from the 20th Century Art Society went to New York. The trip included visits to the studios of Sean Scully, Greg Amenoff, Donald Sultan, and John Coplans as well as to the private collection of art dealer Joe Helman. Amenoff and Scully works entered an Atlanta collection as a result of that trip, and a short time later the Golds acquired Donald Sultan's *Forest Fire* (cat. 42). The purchase was a turning point. New Image painting was the dominant style of the moment and Sultan very much a younger artist of that moment, balancing representational needs with abstract purposes. With its thick tarry surface and carved-on qualities, Sultan's work

clearly stood apart from other works in the Golds' household. Leni put it in the living room where it could be most startling and abrasive. Provocation as a value in contemporary art began to be a quality she savored.

Leni had her own take on these trips, as she did on shows at the High. She worked like an independent curator, checking opinions with collectors and curators, both in town and out. Stefan Edlis, a leading collector in Chicago, became one of the people she consulted on a regular basis, along with other Chicago dealers and collectors. Her learning was based on person-to-person relationships and the opinions of those she respected, as well as her own assiduous looking.

Activities in the 20th Century Art Society also picked up. Mark and Judith Taylor commissioned a wall drawing by Sol LeWitt within a year of the completion of the new building. A 20th Century Art Acquisition Fund was launched, and a Susan Rothenberg drawing acquired as the first purchase of the Fund. Leni by then had relinquished the reins of the 20th Century Art Society but was the first chairman of the Fund. She made a constant push for acquisition funds for the High.

Leni's next major purchase was a work on paper by Anselm Kiefer with straw collaged onto the surface. With that acquisition in 1986, Leni fully emerged as a collector. Although later she purchased a more important Kiefer work, *Brunhilde Sleeps* (cat. 18), the drawing had an enormous impact. The only Kiefer in Atlanta, it was a pilgrimage object. Leni knew that what she was doing was important for Atlanta, and she found new purpose in the rapid evolution of her taste, as witnessed by the Kiefer. Matching it in bravado was the Golds' next acquisition, a painting on black velvet by Julian Schnabel, *She Mistook Kindness for Weakness* (cat. 36).

I left Atlanta in the summer of 1986 to become director of the Speed Art Museum in Louisville, Kentucky. In the period between 1984 and 1986, Leni became fully contemporary in her taste. Her horizons extended to European art, and she was actively involved in a dialogue with art of the moment. She began to ask whether the High would be interested in what she was buying—works of art beyond the reach of the Museum's resources. Within the year the Golds acquired work by Nancy Graves (cat. 10), Donald Judd (cat. 14), Anish Kapoor (cat. 15), Mimmo

Paladino (cat. 33), Joel Shapiro (cat. 39), and a second work by Donald Sultan (cat. 43). She and Burt were shortly to leave Rembrandt Road and move to an apartment that served as a showcase for the burgeoning collection.

Leni was not a collector primarily motivated by the ideas inherent in works of art. She never bought into conceptualism as a style or as something to acquire, nor could she see the attractions of self-taught artists. Her taste, as it evolved in the years from 1980 to 1986, became searching and engaged, rejoicing in the new. She valued the honesty of contemporary art more than its mystery, and she valued her own commitment to that honesty. At its heart, her taste was profoundly humanist and celebrated what is most profoundly human in all of us—both craftsmanship and risk, profundity and plainspokenness, the visual language of meaning and imagination.

What do patrons do? At the High Museum of Art, Lenore Gold asked for vision and she pushed to make it happen. She trained her own eye and taste, and encouraged others to do the same. She put great faith in the Museum staff, and she connected her collecting with the Museum's and encouraged others as well to see the Museum as the nexus for a lively community engagement with contemporary art of lasting value. She was not always someone to take a simple yes for an answer. Looking back, I think she was always right.

1. Gudmund Vigtel, preface, *Drawings in Georgia Collections,* by Peter Morrin and Eric Zafran (Atlanta: High Museum of Art, 1981), p. 5
2. These commissions were preceded by the decoration of the Omni Hotel by Genevieve Arnold in the 1970s and commissions unveiled at Hartsfield International Airport in 1980: artists included were Benny Andrews, Stephen Antonakos, Lynda Benglis, Santo Bruno, Houston Conwill, Richard Friedberg, Sam Gilliam, David Hammons, Margaret Koscielny, Andy Nasisse, Curtis Patterson, Michael Siede, Richard Smith, and Phyllis Thompson.

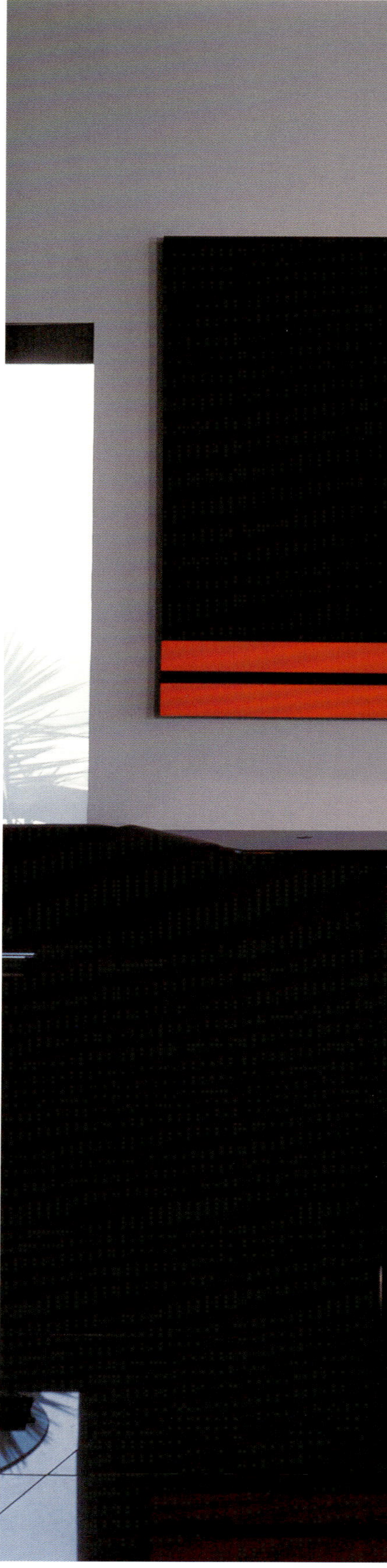

Dining room, Park Place, ca. 1995

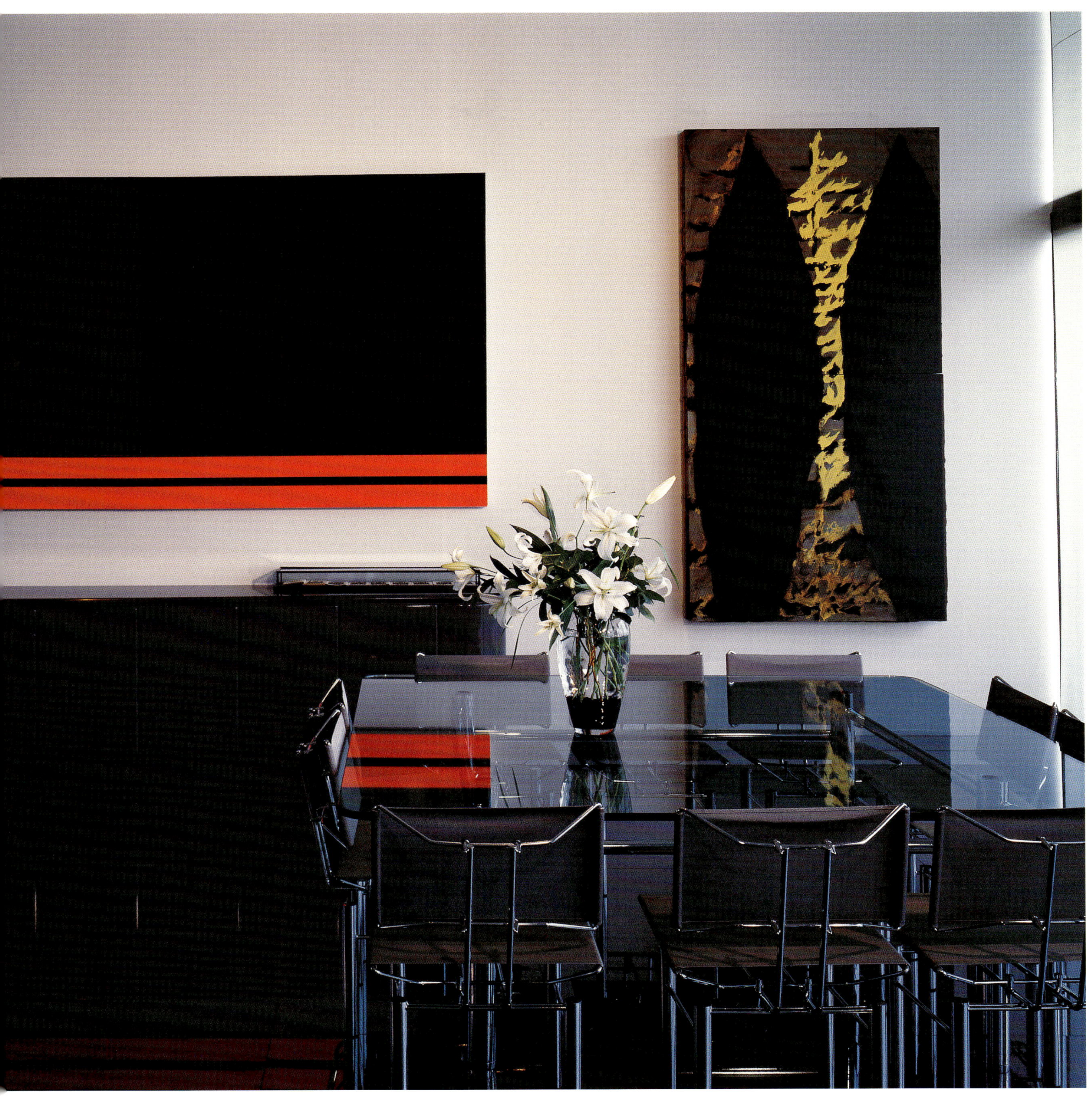

CATALOGUE

George Segal, *The Blue Door,* cat. 37 (detail)

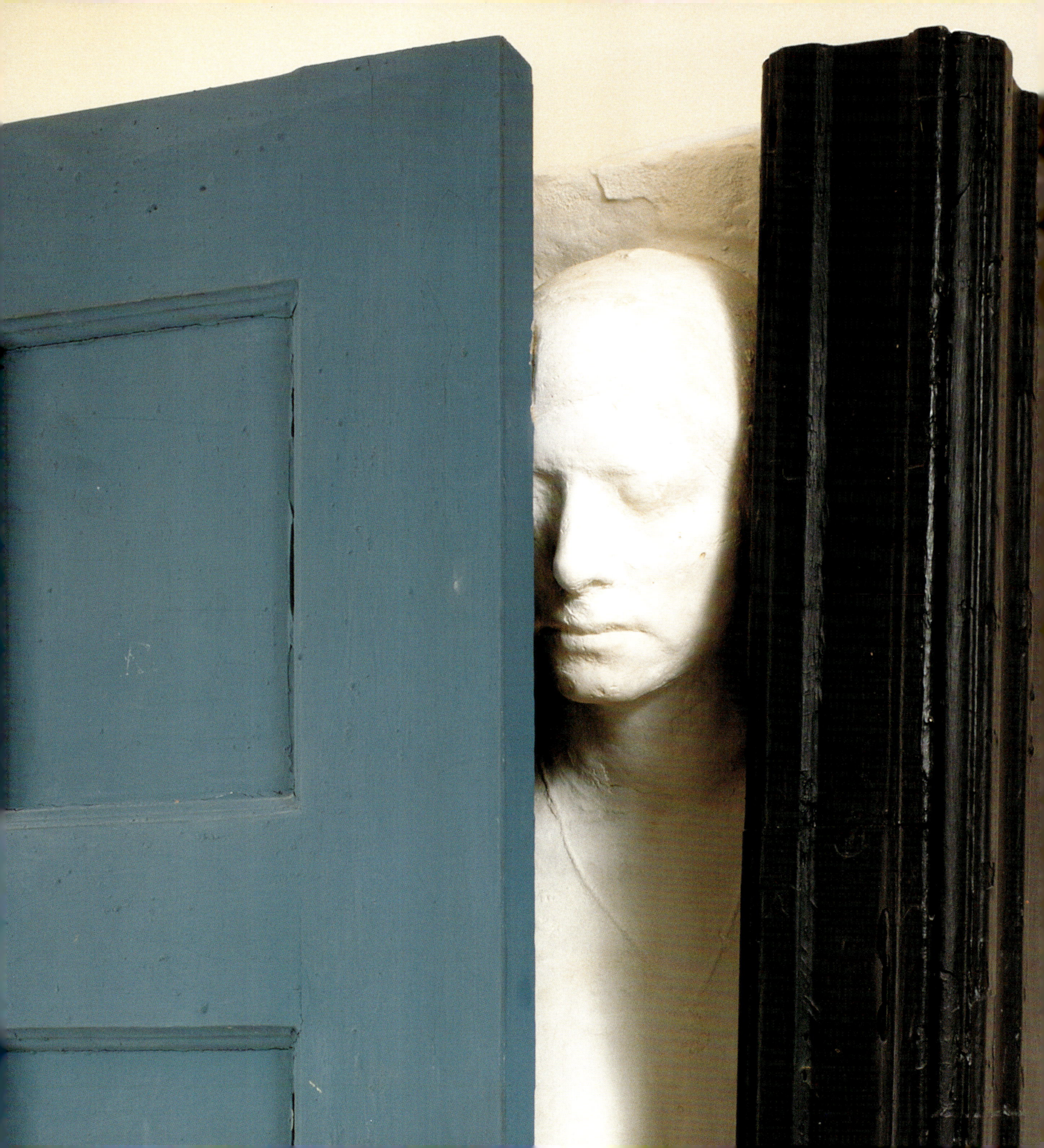

RICHARD ARTSCHWAGER

American, born 1923

Volcano, 1986
Acrylic on Celotex and wood
33¼ × 35½ inches
Collection of Burton Gold

Richard Artschwager came to international prominence in the 1960s. His "pseudo-furniture" —sculptures that sought to approximate factory-made consumer goods but specifically designed not to serve any practical function—explored many of the issues central to Pop Art and shared that movement's ironic tone. Throughout his long career, Artschwager has critiqued contemporary culture, revealing his mordant wit and preoccupation with the conceptual underpinnings of art. For example, he might construct a table from wood, laminate it with white plastic, then paint an elaborate wood grain over the laminate in order to point out the absurd ways that simulated materials have displaced real things and thus question our conventions of representation. Foremost, Artschwager's is an art about art, an investigation of how artworks take on and convey meaning. His works are never composed exclusively around formal concerns but rather are designed to foil, and thus to call attention to, the expectations and assumptions of viewers. The artist continually reminds us that meaning in a work of art is not stable but conventionally determined. He seeks to subtly but deliberately change the context in which we see an object in order to shift our understanding of it. "Sculpture is for the touch. Painting is for the eye," he says. "I wanted to make a sculpture for the eye and a painting for the touch."[1] Above all, he strives to make physical objects that engage the intellect.

A principal strategy in Artschwager's work is what he calls "the truncation of the senses," a means of refocusing the viewer's attention on unexpected details by removal of others. "First you chop sound away from the field of experience,"

he explains. "Next, you see that the image doesn't move. So it separates out. The picture becomes a disjunction. And the key to the sublime for me is this elimination of some of the senses to get to a strengthening, a *burning* of the other senses. Something usual is left out so that the rest is heightened. And that's what I'm trying to do: give people beauty through abridgement."[2]

Volcano provides a prime example of this approach. It is a fairly small painting set in an imposing black frame, actually part of the work, which clearly separates it from its surroundings. The image depicted within the frame resembles a rudimentary drawing of a landscape. The artist has rendered the scene in pale shades of gray that are further diffused by the crusty surface on which it is painted. Because of the painting's muted hues, the small spot of orange at the mouth of the erupting volcano serves as the focus of the composition long before the viewer deciphers the subject. The textured surface on which Artschwager paints is Celotex, a material used for soundproofing. With his painting, the artist has reduced a tremendous force of nature, a volcano, to a manageable size, and through his choice of materials indicates that he has further silenced it. In so doing, he raises questions about the tradition of landscape painting and its relationship to the human desire to conquer nature.

Carrie Przybilla

1. Quoted in Steven Henry Madoff, "Richard Artschwager's Sleight of Mind," *ARTnews* 87, no. 1 (January 1988), p. 116.
2. Quoted in ibid., p. 118.

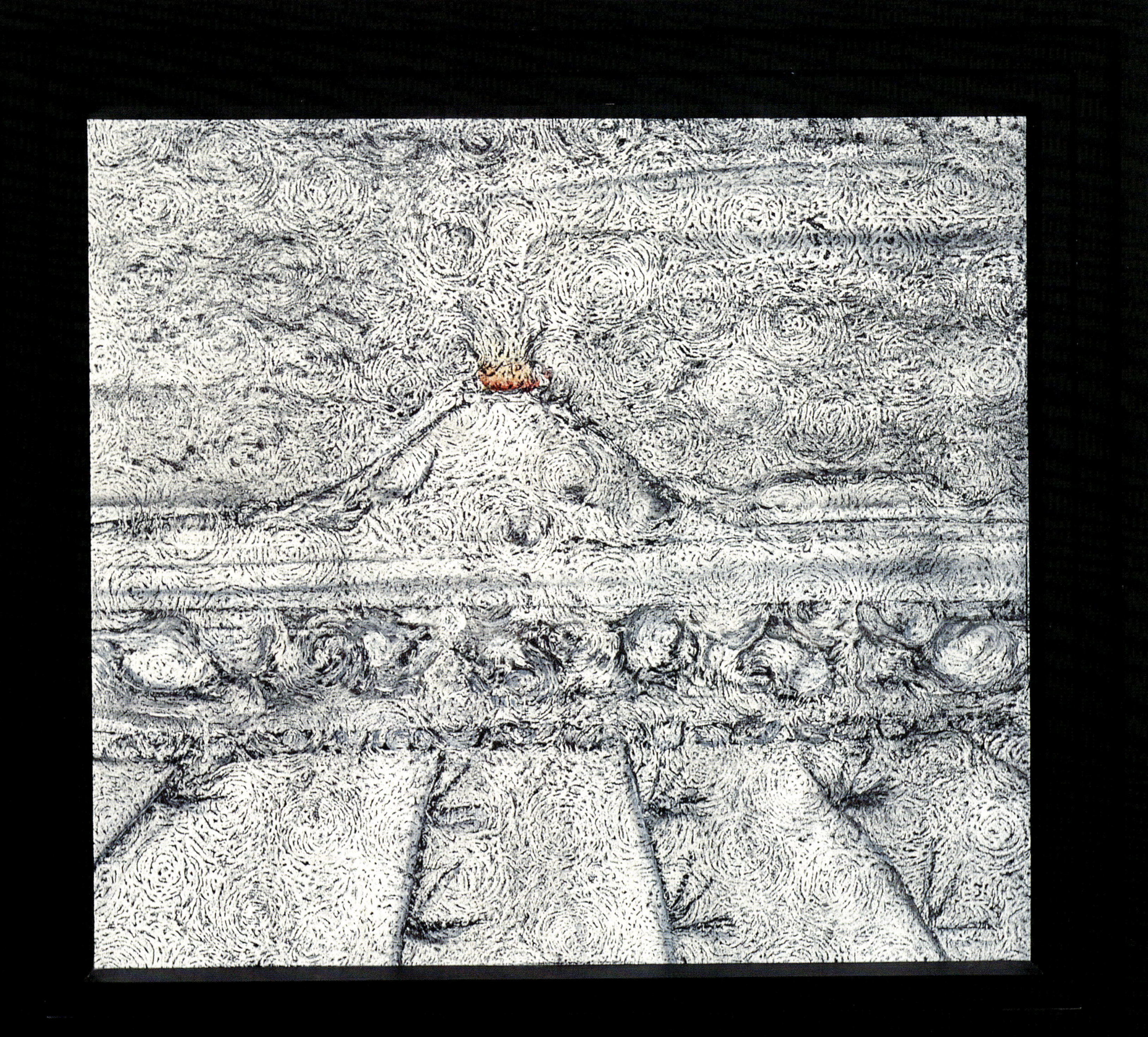

CHRISTIAN BOLTANSKI

French, born 1944

Monument/Odessa, 1990

11 photographs, 3 tin biscuit boxes, 68 light bulbs,
  glass, and electrical cords
Overall: 122 × 48 × 8⅝ inches
High Museum of Art, The Lenore and Burton Gold
  Collection of 20th-Century Art, 1999.109

Through his photographic installations,
Christian Boltanski probes the intertwined themes
of childhood, memory, and death. He views
memories of the beginning of life and rituals that
memorialize its end as reflections of our understanding of history and, indeed, of life itself. As
he has pointed out, "there have only been three
or four subjects in the whole history of art. Death
is one of them."[1] Given the themes of his work, it
is tempting to assume that Boltanski's personal
history is its subject: born in Paris to Jewish parents just days after the liberation of that city during World War II, he grew up acutely aware of
the Holocaust and its aftermath. In fact, Boltanski
is far more interested in collective memory than
in the details of his own experience and has
stated, "I don't believe in autobiography. The
only possible autobiographies are those that are
about everyone."[2]

Photography—modern memory's chief tool—
has long served as Boltanski's primary medium.
He has called photographic portraits "a memory
of somebody who has disappeared,"[3] recognizing
that any single picture, like memory itself, can
capture only fleeting moments. The biscuit tins
the artist has included in his work since 1970 similarly represent the vagaries of memory. Battered
and worn, they clearly have histories, but their
contents are inaccessible to the viewer. Boltanski
frequently uses such ordinary objects, particularly
those with past lives, because he wishes "to take
something simple, ugly, insignificant, or humble,

and transform it, giving it a magical, mystical dimension. I think the beauty in art is the dispro-
portion of the poverty of means. In this poverty, I
search for and obtain a spiritual richness."[4]

While not an orthodox follower of any faith,
Boltanski has a deep sense of the sacred and a
respect for ritual that manifests itself in his work,
particularly in the series of "monuments" he began creating in the mid-1980s. Just as his work
questions the nature of memory, Boltanski's con-
ception of a monument challenges traditional notions of what constitutes a proper memorial and
anchors his seemingly ad hoc installations:

> If you make a monument in stone, everyone will
> soon forget what you have commemorated. The
> city will pay for the monument in order to forget
> it. What I wanted to do was to make a monu-
> ment that would have to be remade each month,
> using very fragile materials. . . . Of course, the
> monument would fall down and have to be con-
> tinually reconstructed. If at any time it disap-
> peared, it would mean that times had changed,
> and the reasons for its existence were forgotten.
> The only possible monuments are those that must
> be continually re-made, that require a continuous
> engagement, so that people will remember.[5]

This work is a typical Boltanski monument. It
consists of ten portrait photographs of children
hung above three biscuit boxes that protrude
from the wall like shelves. The portraits are rendered anonymous by the close cropping of the

images, which seem blurry and may have dark-
ened with age. The identities of these children
are further shrouded by a tangle of electrical
cords that drape around and in front of the pictures, supplying power to dozens of small electrical lights that encircle the installation. Seemingly
intended to illuminate the display, instead the
bare bulbs create a glare across the surfaces of
the photographs that makes them even more
difficult to discern. The overall effect is that of a
shrine or altar that memorializes a barely remembered, inarticulable loss.

Carrie Przybilla

1. Boltanski, "Christian Boltanski: Carrion, Clown and
   Jew," interview by Georgia Marsh, in Lynn Gumpert,
   Reconstitution (London: Whitechapel Art Gallery;
   Eindhoven, Netherlands: Stedelijk van Abbemuseum;
   Grenoble, France: Musée de Grenoble, 1990), p. 20.
2. Boltanski, "Christian Boltanski: A Conversation with
   Leslie Camhi," interview by Leslie Camhi, *The Print
   Collector's Newsletter* 23, no. 6 (January/February 1993),
   p. 202.
3. Boltanski, "Sans-Souci: Christian Boltanski Interviewed,"
   interview by Mark Durden and Lydia Papadimitriou,
   Creative Camera 315 (April/May 1992), p. 22.
4. Boltanski, "Christian Boltanski," interview by Demos-
   thénes Davvetas, *Flash Art* 124 (October/November
   1985), p. 83.
5. Boltanski, Camhi interview, p. 204.

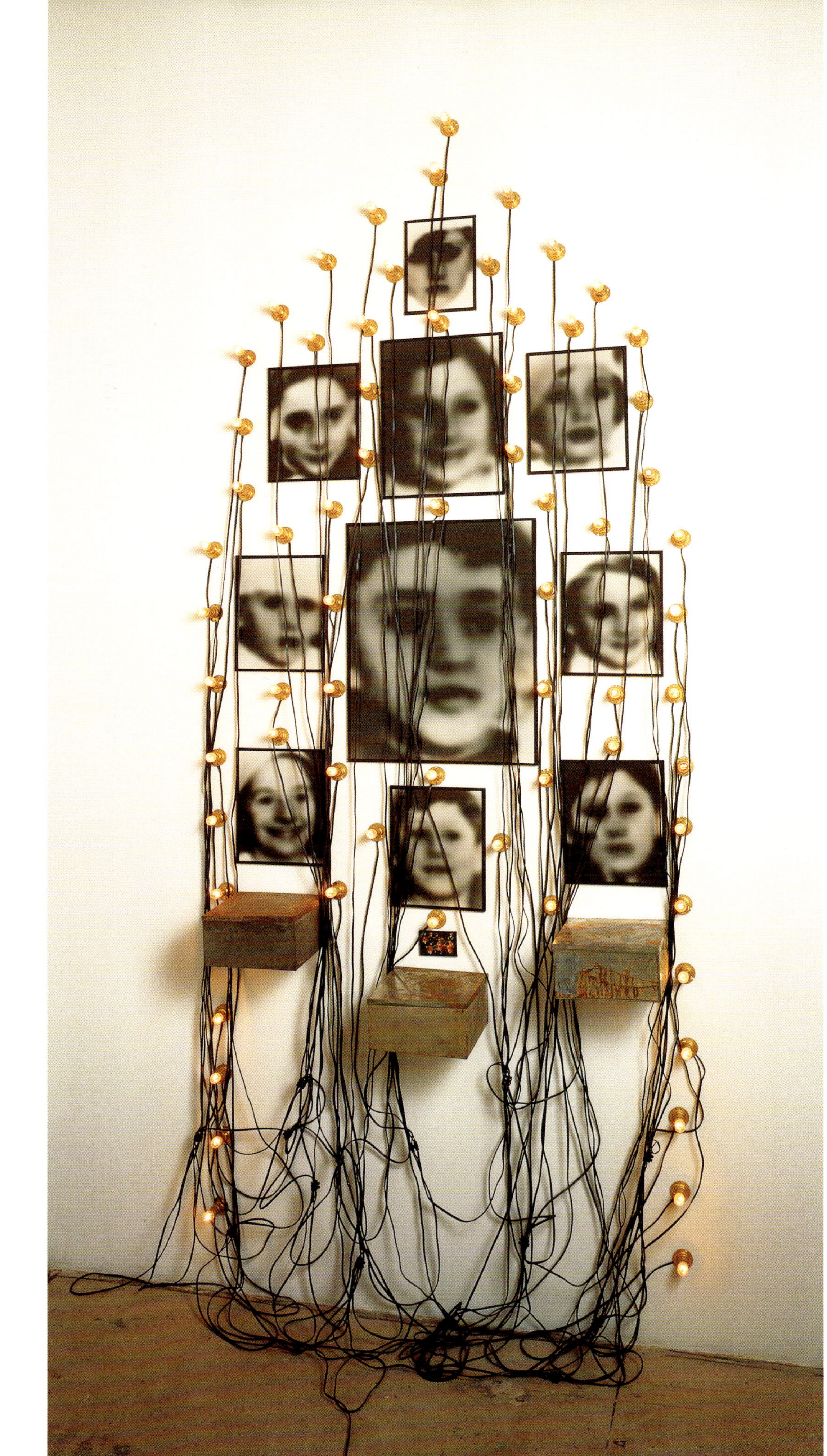

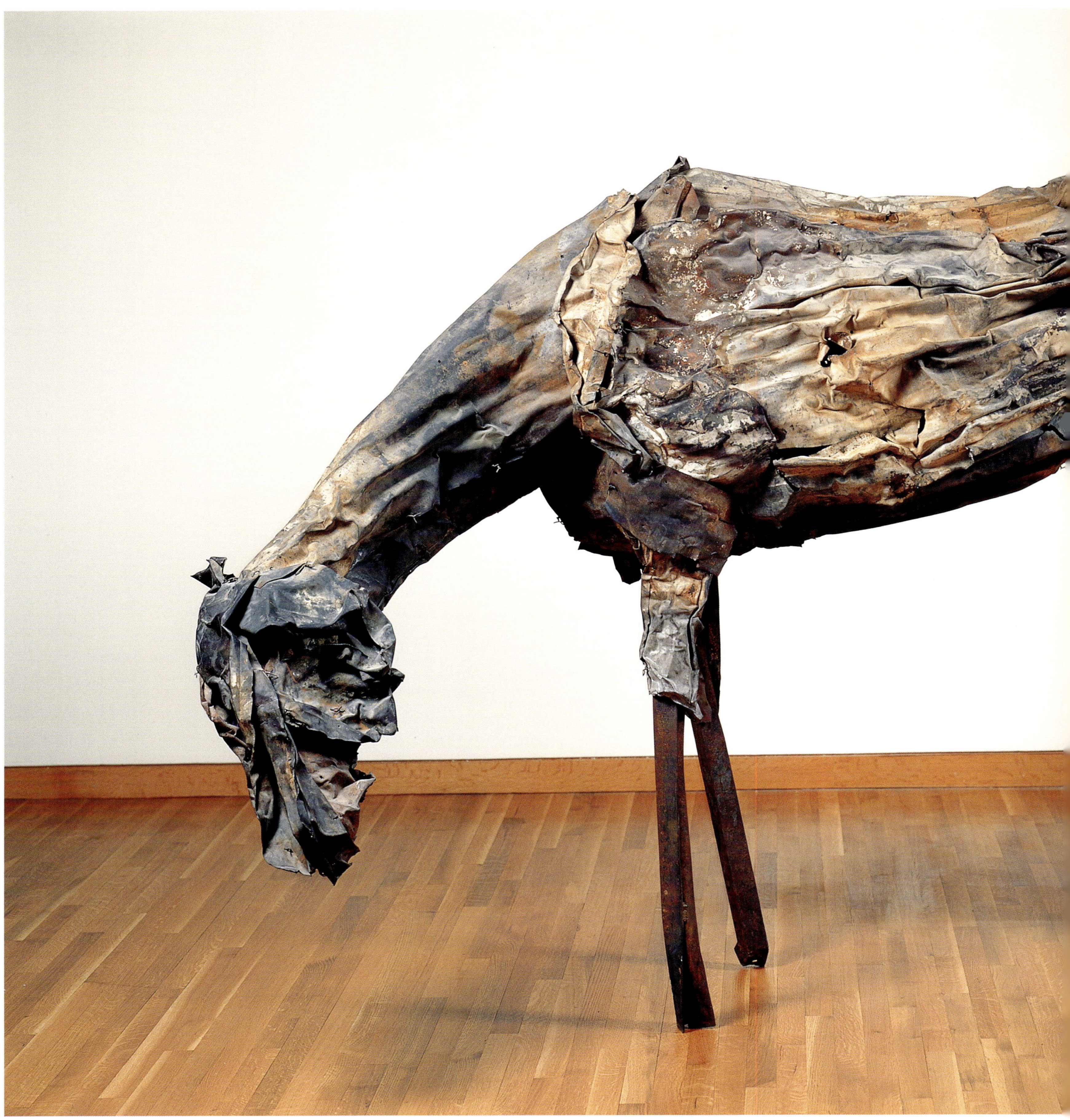

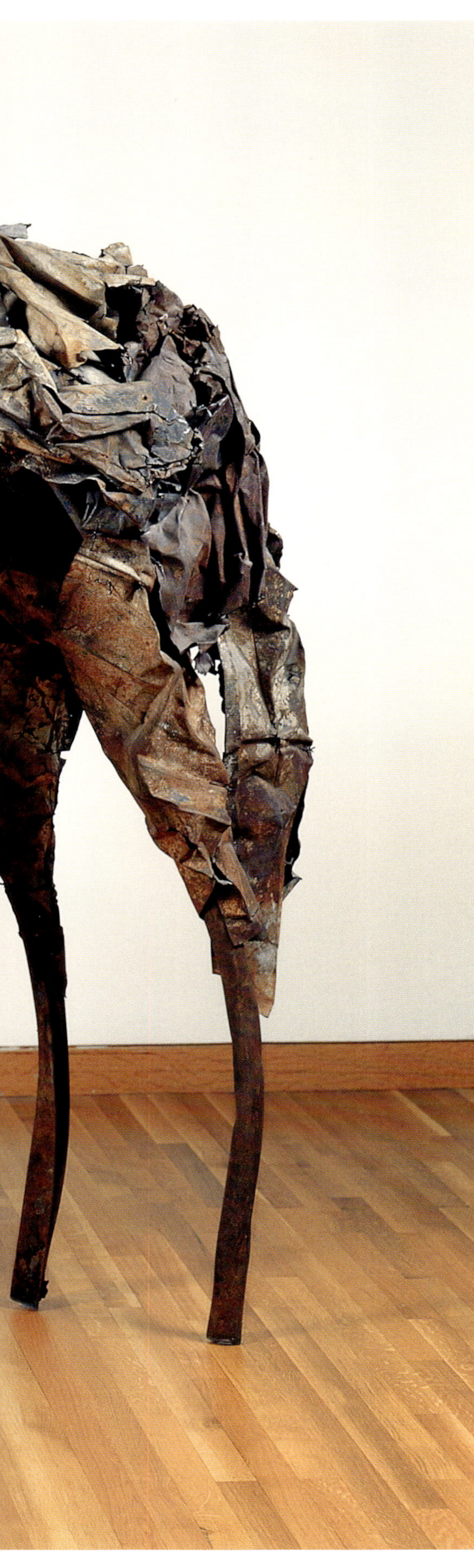

DEBORAH BUTTERFIELD

American, born 1949

Untitled (#3-85), 1985
Burned and crushed steel and barbed wire
73 × 99 × 45 inches
High Museum of Art, The Lenore and Burton Gold
    Collection of 20th-Century Art, 1999.110

Deborah Butterfield began to use the horse as the basis for her sculpture in 1972, while still a graduate student. An equestrian for most of her life, she has chosen her subject not because of its noble artistic ancestors, such as the steeds found in the Elgin Marbles and the works of Géricault and Degas, but because she admires the animals themselves. The artist explains that "while horses are not intelligent at doing things that people do or that dogs do, they are very intelligent at doing things that horses do, and I'm interested in what that has to teach me."[1]

Butterfield sculpted her first horse while searching for an artistic surrogate for herself. "I wanted to make art about myself and my life," she says, "but I did not want to use the human figure."[2] Although they originally served as a form of self-portraiture, Butterfield's horses have developed into meditations on the human condition. The artist is not interested in depicting perfect equine specimens, such as Black Beauty or Pie from *National Velvet.* Her horses have been called the Ralph Kramdens of horseflesh;[3] they evoke a commonness with which we can readily identify. The work in the Gold Collection is typical. This life-size horse stands with neck extended, head lowered, and ears flattened in a posture that suggests submission and caution, even as it beseeches the viewer's attention. The crushed, rusting steel and barbed wire from which it is constructed reinforce the sense that this animal is bereft, decrepit, and world-weary.

Her equestrian experience has taught Butterfield a great deal about the physical structure of horses. She notes that in "training a dressage horse you're making a sculpture, because you're redistributing the muscle structure of the horse. I find myself building my sculptural horses the way I'd like to build my real horses."[4] Although life-size since the beginning, her sculptures have evolved through a variety of materials. The first series of horses was made of plaster. Soon, Butterfield turned to sticks and mud, which eventually gave way to other found materials, all having implied histories and distinct visual connotations. Although her materials may be recognizable, the artist emphasizes their role as part of the greater whole that she is creating. This ability to create a coherent image that captures the subtleties of a wide range of emotions demonstrates Butterfield's mastery of both her materials and subject.

Humans have long admired the horse, holding it up as a symbol of strength, grace, nobility, and freedom. Although Butterfield loves horses, in her sculptures they are simply a means to an end. Ultimately, she says, "The point about my work is the empathy of shared gesture between horse and human. My work is about creating the empathy so that we can step into the form—if only for a split second—and have feeling for the 'other.' Most of the world is 'other,' and once we can step out of 'self,' we are more likely to be able to do so again."[5]

Carrie Przybilla

1. Quoted in Marcia Tucker, "Equestrian Mysteries," *Art in America* 77, no. 6 (June 1989), p. 156.
2. Quoted in Thomas H. Garver, *Mind & Beast: Contemporary Artists and the Animal Kingdom* (Wausau, Wis.: Leigh Yawkey Woodson Art Museum, 1992), p. 24.
3. Richard Martin, "A Horse Perceived by Sighted Persons: New Sculptures by Deborah Butterfield," *Arts* 61, no. 5 (January 1987), p. 75.
4. Quoted in Tucker, p. 156.
5. Quoted in Garver, p. 25.

ALEXANDER CALDER

American, 1898–1976

a. **Untitled,** 1942

Gouache on paper
22 × 30 inches
Collection of Pamela Gold Alexander

b. **Untitled,** 1942

Gouache on paper
21¾ × 30 inches
Collection of Janice Gold Dietz

c. **Untitled,** 1942

Gouache on paper
22 × 29⅞ inches
Collection of Lauren G. Grien

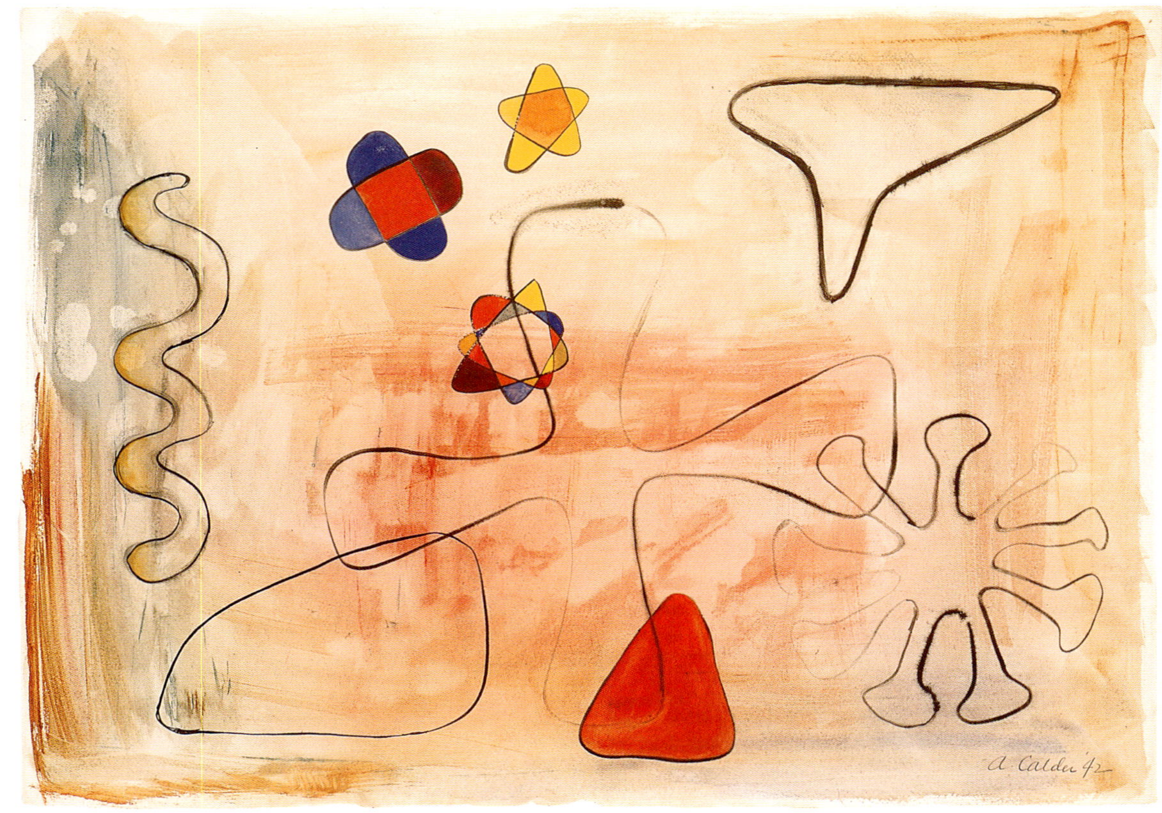

The son of a painter and a sculptor, Alexan-der Calder was encouraged in creative pursuits from early childhood. He did not receive any formal artistic training, however, until he was in his mid-twenties, after first establishing a career as a mechanical engineer in New York. There he enrolled in evening classes at the Art Students' League and studied with such illustrious teachers as George Luks and John Sloan. An excellent draftsman, Calder was particularly noted for his ability to convey a sense of movement with a single unbroken line and for his whimsical series of small wire sculptures depicting circus performers. Although the artist would later become famous for his sculptural works, their foundation in his talent for drawing is indisputable.

Calder quickly outgrew the conservative confines of the Art Students' League, and in 1926 he made his first trip to Paris, then the center of the art world. During a series of extended visits to France over the next decade, he actively participated in the European vanguard, receiving par-ticular encouragement from Joan Miró, Marcel Duchamp, and Jean Arp. Ardently committed to non-representational art at a time when most of his compatriots were struggling to comprehend abstraction, Calder was one of the few Americans invited to become a member of the Abstraction-Création group, which included Arp, Jean Hélion, and Piet Mondrian, and he regularly showed his work alongside theirs. Before the outbreak of World War II, the relationship of his biomorphic forms to those of Miró, Arp, and the other abstract Surrealists was widely recognized. This affinity was underscored in 1942, when he was one of a handful of Americans included in the pivotal New York exhibition *First Papers of Surrealism.*

These three gouache drawings from that same year clearly demonstrate Calder's debt to Surrealism. Although primarily a sculptor, he worked in a variety of media throughout his career. The artist said he particularly enjoyed working in gouache because "it goes fast and one can surprise oneself."[1] Gouache, an opaque watercolor, provides a palette of bold colors but, unlike oil paint, dries rapidly. In each of these drawings, hieroglyphic shapes float past one another in a space of indeterminate depth. The forms in cat. 4b particularly reveal the influence of Miró in the large asterisk at the center of the composition and the two small black shapes suggesting figures in the lower left. The spatters of paint across this work introduce an element of chance, a prime Surrealist strategy for tapping the subconscious. Calder avoids the dark, ominous tone of much Surrealism, however, choosing bold colors and energetic compositions that seem cheerful, despite the looming war.

Carrie Przybilla

1. Quoted in Jean Lipman, *Calder's Universe* (New York: Whitney Museum of American Art and The Viking Press, 1976), p. 119.

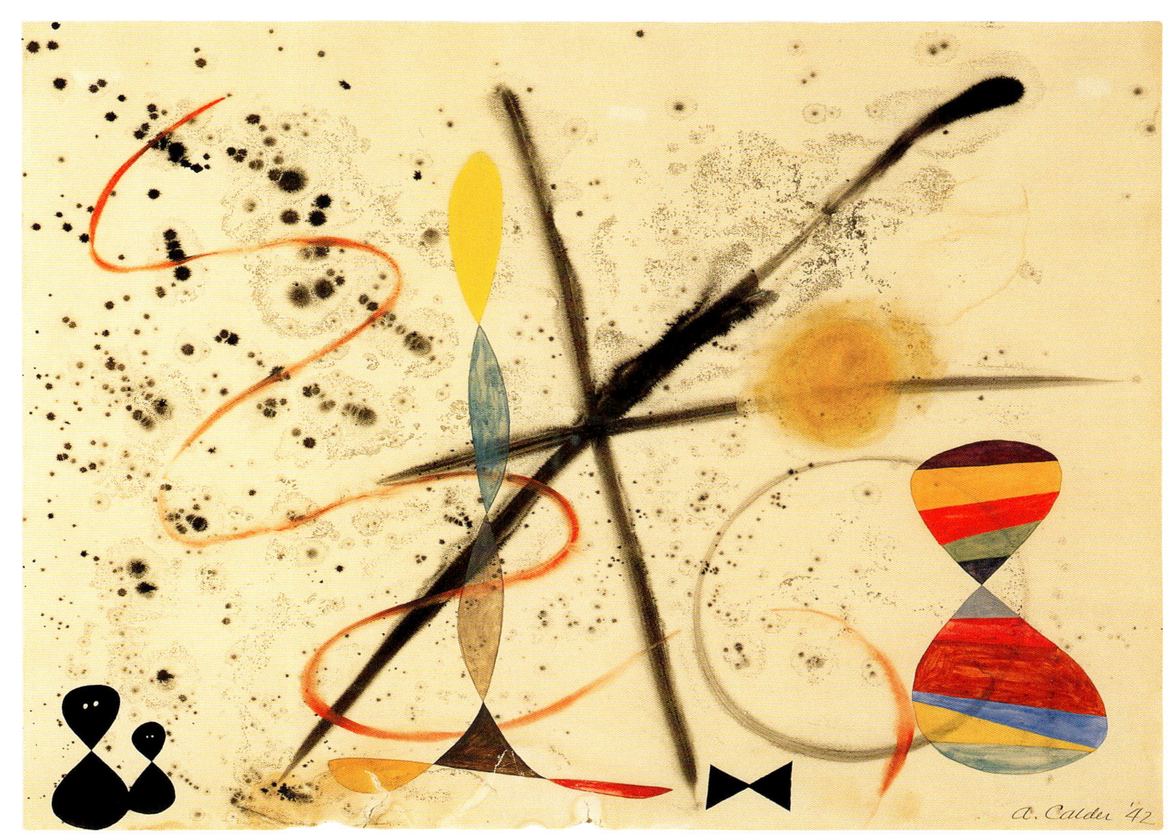

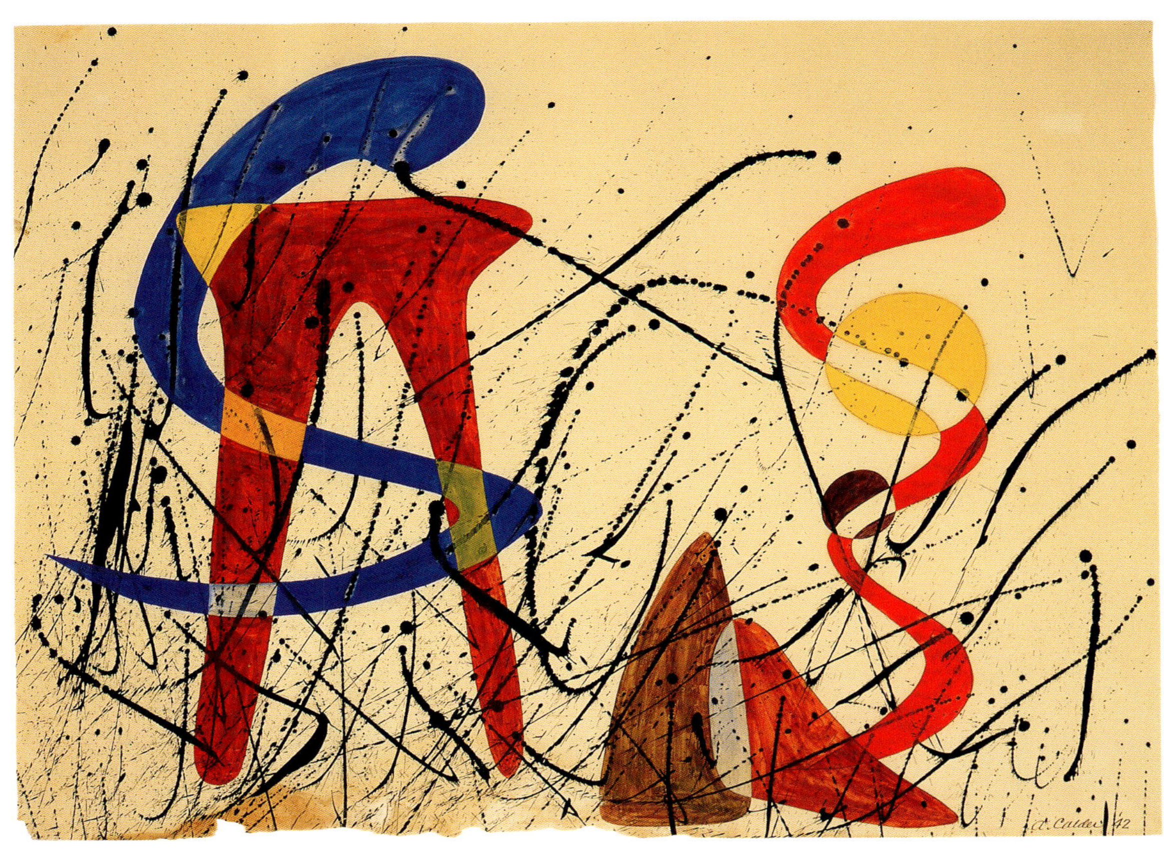

ALEXANDER CALDER

American, 1898–1976

Untitled, 1960
Enamel on metal
18½ × 29 inches (diameter: 34 inches)
Collection of Joanne Gold

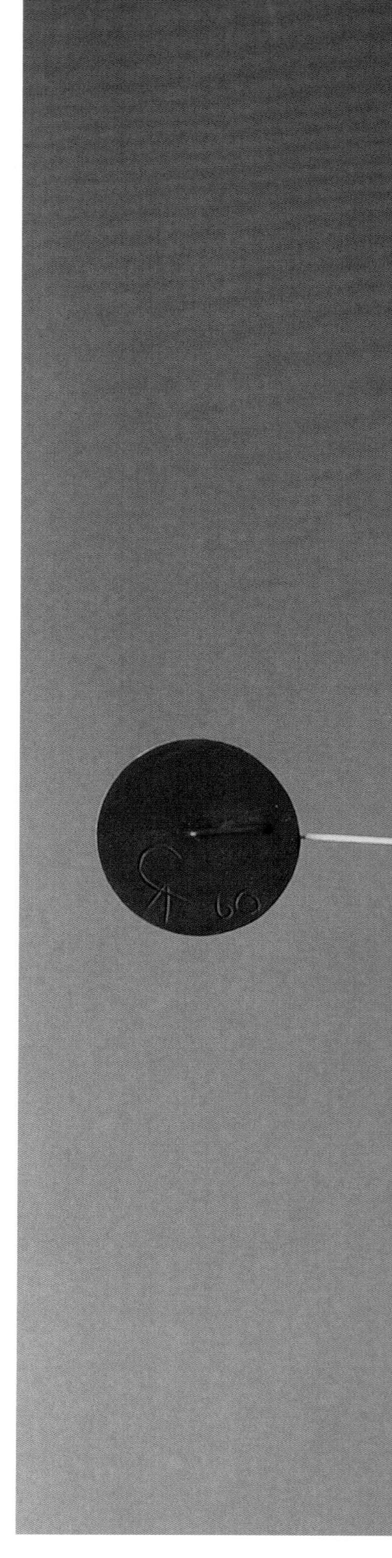

The radical nature of Alexander Calder's sculpture is hard to grasp a quarter-century after the artist's death. The mobile, which he invented as a form of sculpture, is now ubiquitous, found over cribs and in gift shops everywhere. This does not detract from his key achievement in twentieth-century art, however. Calder's mobiles enlarged the vocabulary of sculpture even as modernist construction was still inventing itself. His innovation is part of the reason that the terms "sculpture" and "statue" ceased to be interchangeable.

Calder comprehended and embraced abstraction quickly. During a visit to Piet Mondrian's studio in Paris, he saw the ever-changing compositions the Dutch artist created by pinning squares of colored paper to the wall, and he imagined the squares moving in space. "Why not plastic forms in motion?" he thought. "Not a simple translatory or rotary motion, but several motions of different types, speeds and amplitudes composing to make a resultant whole. Just as one can compose colors, or forms, so one can compose motions."[1] Calder immediately put his training as a mechanical engineer to work, assembling abstract compositions from pieces of shaped and painted metal suspended on thin wires or cords. Although they seem to be put together intuitively, the mobiles succeed because of the artist's thoughtful deployment of static and kinetic elements. Each responds to the faintest air current while simultaneously counterbalancing the motion of each of the other elements. The color and placement of each component take full advantage of the effects of changing light created by the movement.

Although Calder produced his first mobile in 1931, his works were not so dubbed until 1932, by Marcel Duchamp. "I asked him," Calder later recounted, "what sort of a name I could give these things and he at once produced 'mobile.'" Calder was delighted by the term because "in addition to something that moves, in French it also means motive."

This untitled mobile was produced nearly thirty years later. The artist by that time had made a wide range of sculptures, from heroic to Lilliputian in scale. Although this work is relatively modest in size, it reveals key elements of Calder's approach. The cascading arrangement of repeated circles at first seems very straightforward, but as the circles bob and weave to counterbalance one another, the overall composition becomes complex. The viewer readily senses Calder's love for supersaturated primary colors and his particular affection for red, despite his contention that he used color "just for differentiation." By highlighting the arms of this mobile with brilliant yellow, the artist focuses attention on their movements and the ways they activate the space, achieving his goal of "four-dimensional drawing."

Carrie Przybilla

1. All quotations from Arnauld Pierre, *Motion, Emotion: The Art of Alexander Calder* (New York: O'Hara Gallery, 1999), unpaginated.

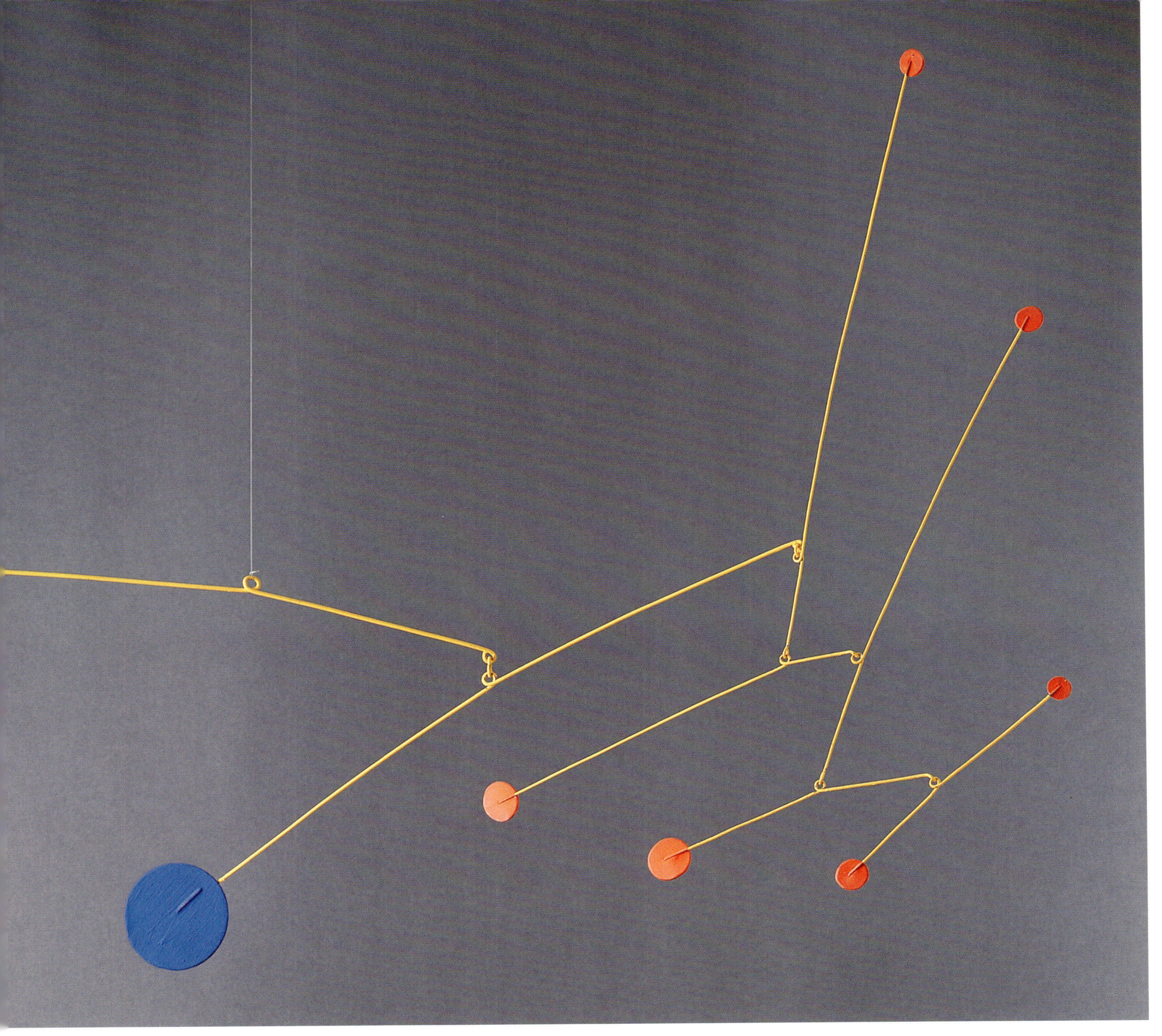

JOHN CHAMBERLAIN

American, born 1927

Monkey Fist, 1976
Enamel on steel and chromium-plated steel
39 × 16½ × 24 inches
Promised gift of Burton Gold to the High Museum of
  Art for The Lenore and Burton Gold Collection of
  20th-Century Art

Throughout John Chamberlain's prolific career, his work has resisted pigeonholing and defied stereotypes. Chamberlain does not identify with a specific movement, although some critics have grouped him with the Abstract Expressionists because of his use of color, spontaneous energy, and concern for light and surface. Others associate the artist with the Pop Art movement because he has appropriated the automobile into his work, incorporating a familiar emblem of American popular culture. Perhaps the closest comparisons lie with Kurt Schwitters, Marcel Duchamp, and David Smith, who through their assemblages and sculptures breathed new life into the discarded.

Born in 1927 in Rochester, Indiana, Chamberlain grew up in Chicago. Following a stint in the Navy, he attended hairdressing school under the GI Bill before entering The School of the Art Institute of Chicago in 1951. By 1955, he was enrolled at Black Mountain College, where the literary emphasis—particularly of poets Charles Olson and Robert Creeley—ultimately fed Chamberlain and freed him, profoundly affecting his method of making art. He later realized its impact:

> At Black Mountain College, everybody read books. I read these things and when I saw a word I liked, I'd isolate it. I'd write it down. So I had this collection of words that I liked to look at. It didn't matter what they meant. . . . I would put them together and come up with an image that was unlike anything you could achieve if

you didn't do it this way. . . . There is material to be seen around you every day. But one day something—some one thing—pops out at you, and you pick it up, and take it over, and you put it somewhere else, and it *fits*, it's just the right thing at the right moment. You can do the same thing with words or with metal.[1]

It is this "fit" that Chamberlain has sought ever since. In 1957 he settled in New York and started to develop his sculpture, exploring the plasticity of steel. He had fashioned his first steel sculptures in 1954, attributing his technique and linear style to David Smith, whose work he had seen in Chicago. Chamberlain continued working in this vein, combining iron rods and found objects to produce a body of curvilinear sculptures. When his supply of metal ran low, he pondered his next step: "I was looking for another material. It occurred to me one day that all this material was just lying all over the place. I saw the material as other people's idea of waste. *Shortstop* was made at Larry Rivers's house [with] material from a 1929 Ford. . . . I took a fender. I didn't want to use it as a fender, so I drove over it a few times to rearrange its shape, which was the beginning of what I now know as *process*."[2]

Made of painted and chromium-plated steel, *Shortstop* launched Chamberlain's career, and the artist began fabricating sculpture from crushed automobile parts, developing and fine-tuning what is now his signature style. He discovered the malleability of steel and employed this feature to

maximum effect. Chamberlain became a habitué
of junkyards, selecting steel fragments because of
shape and color. Relying on both chance and intuition, he cut up, reconfigured, and sometimes
even repainted these elements, relishing their
dings and rough edges and how the components
fit together.

Chamberlain's vocabulary then grew: after
investigating the properties of urethane foam,
paper bags, Plexiglas, polymer resin, and aluminum foil in the late 1960s and early 1970s, he
returned to the idea of twisted, wadded steel,
which even now occupies him with its infinite
possibilities. *Monkey Fist* is an abstract, multicolored wall relief. With its jagged steel elements
merging into a triangular composition, *Monkey
Fist* is more compact and vibrant than its ante-
cedents. The artist has inserted his own exuberant
hand, adding a gestural explosion of color to the
prefabricated industrial paint surface. The joyful
palette and buckled forms work harmoniously in
a vivacious dance that denies gravity and weight.

Trinkett Clark

1. Chamberlain, "Auto/Bio: Conversations with John
   Chamberlain," interview by Julie Sylvester, in *John
   Chamberlain: A Catalogue Raisonné of the Sculpture,
   1954–1985* (New York: Hudson Hills Press in association
   with The Museum of Contemporary Art, Los Angeles,
   1986), p. 11.
2. Ibid., p. 15.

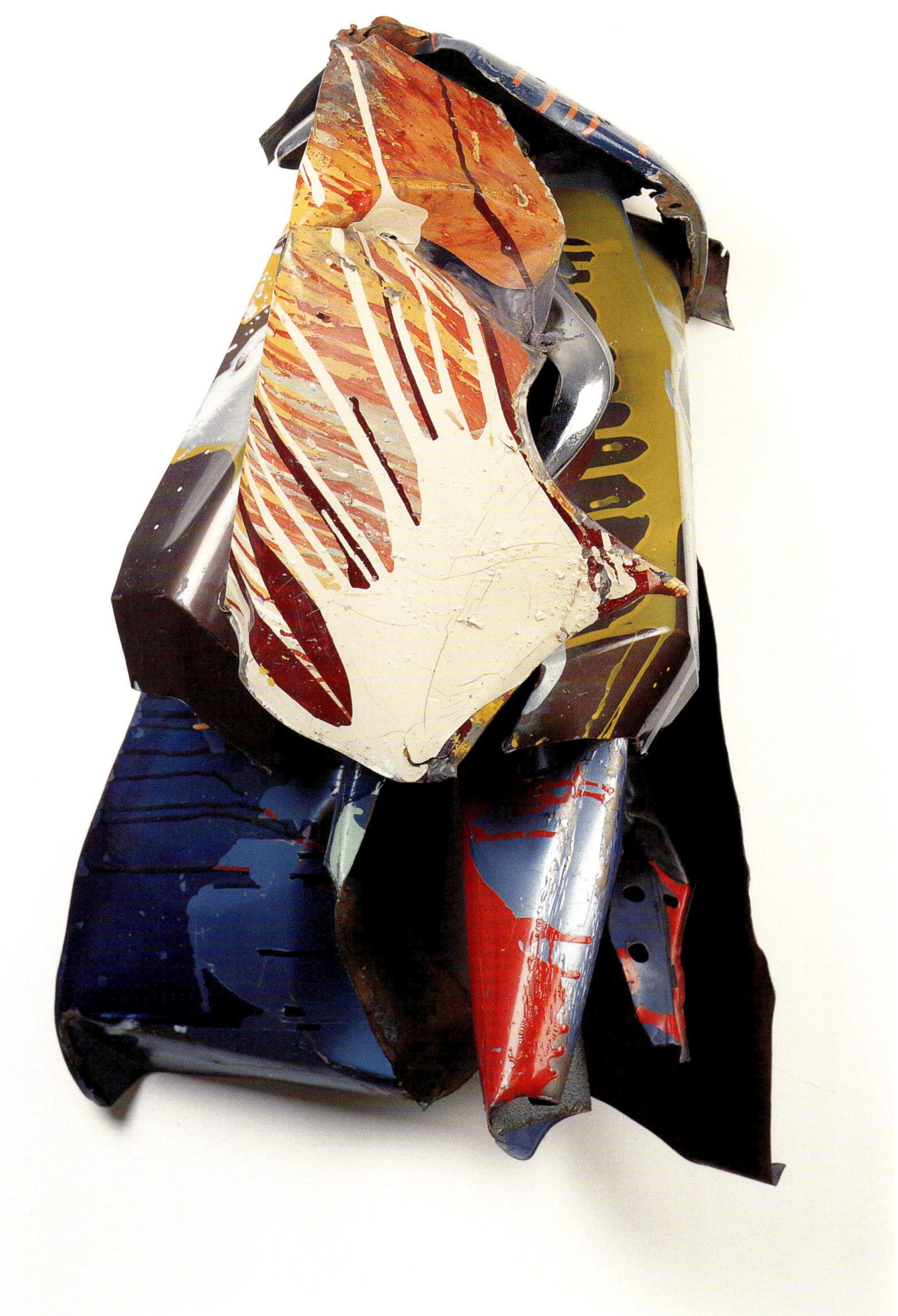

IMOGEN CUNNINGHAM

American, 1883–1976

Datura, ca. 1930

Gelatin silver print
9⅞ × 12¾ inches
High Museum of Art, The Lenore and Burton Gold
   Collection of 20th-Century Art, given in memory
   of Helen B. Fisher, 75.97

What I like to see about a photograph is
everything smoothly in focus.

—Imogen Cunningham[1]

Imogen Cunningham was inspired to begin
taking photographs by the work of Gertrude
Käsebier and was motivated to pursue the art
form on a full-time basis by images she saw in
Camera Work, the photographic quarterly published by Alfred Stieglitz. Beginning in 1901, she
photographed nudes, landscapes, artists, writers,
street vignettes, and botanical still lifes with
distinction. Cunningham was one of America's
pioneers in establishing photography as a fine art
form. She was the first woman to photograph a
male nude. She was a founding member of Group
f64, a San Francisco–based coalition that included
Edward Weston, Willard Van Dyke, Ansel Adams,
and other proponents of straight photography.
She assisted Edward Curtis for two years when he
was compiling his Native American portfolio, and
she later took photographs for *Vanity Fair.*

By 1920 Cunningham's initial interest in soft
pictorial images shifted to close, tightly cropped,
and highly detailed photographs of faces and
plants. Traditionally, scholars have attributed her
work in this manner to the influence of male colleagues, especially Weston, who also saw lyrical,
geometric abstraction in natural objects. More
recent studies of her work suggest that Cunningham may have adopted this approach before
many of her contemporaries; her style emerged
from her conviction that photography should
reflect what the camera does best—render detail,
distill form.[2]

Datura is an example of Cunningham's use of
close-ups to emphasize form, light, and detail.
The stark nature of the bloom's isolation confuses
its scale and thus its identity. The play of sunlight
and shadow, shape and pattern, angle and dark-
ened surroundings pushes toward abstraction.
Datura represents Cunningham's tendency to
hone in on the lush, sensuous properties of
natural forms. Such floral images brought her
international acclaim and rendered her the photographic equivalent to American modernist
Georgia O'Keeffe, best known for her large,
precise paintings of single flowers. Cunningham
probed into the deep interior of the flower's cup
and exposed its most intimate curves, folds, and
textures without obscuring its identity in severe
abstraction. The more intense her scrutiny, the
more the flower assumed qualities of flesh and
being.

In the midst of making portraits of an amaryl-
lis, a magnolia, an iris, a pair of calla lillies, and
even a datura, Cunningham maintained the ability to turn her lens toward human subjects. They
were the basis of her formal understanding and
the key to her psychological insight: "Photography began for me with people and no matter
what interest I have given [to other things] I have
never totally deserted the bigger significance of
human life."[3]

Amalia Amaki

1. Quoted in *Portrait of Imogen,* dir. Meg Partridge,
   28 min., New Day Films, 1987, videocassette.
2. Jacqueline M. Pontello, "Photo Finish," *Southwest Art*
   (May 1993), p. 193; and Andy Grundberg, "Photography
   View: Revisiting a Modernist Pioneer and a Poet of Urban Life," *New York Times,* 5 January 1986, sec. 2, p. 29.
3. Quoted in Richard Lorenz, *Imogen Cunningham, Ideas
   Without End* (San Francisco: Chronicle Books, 1993), p. 9.

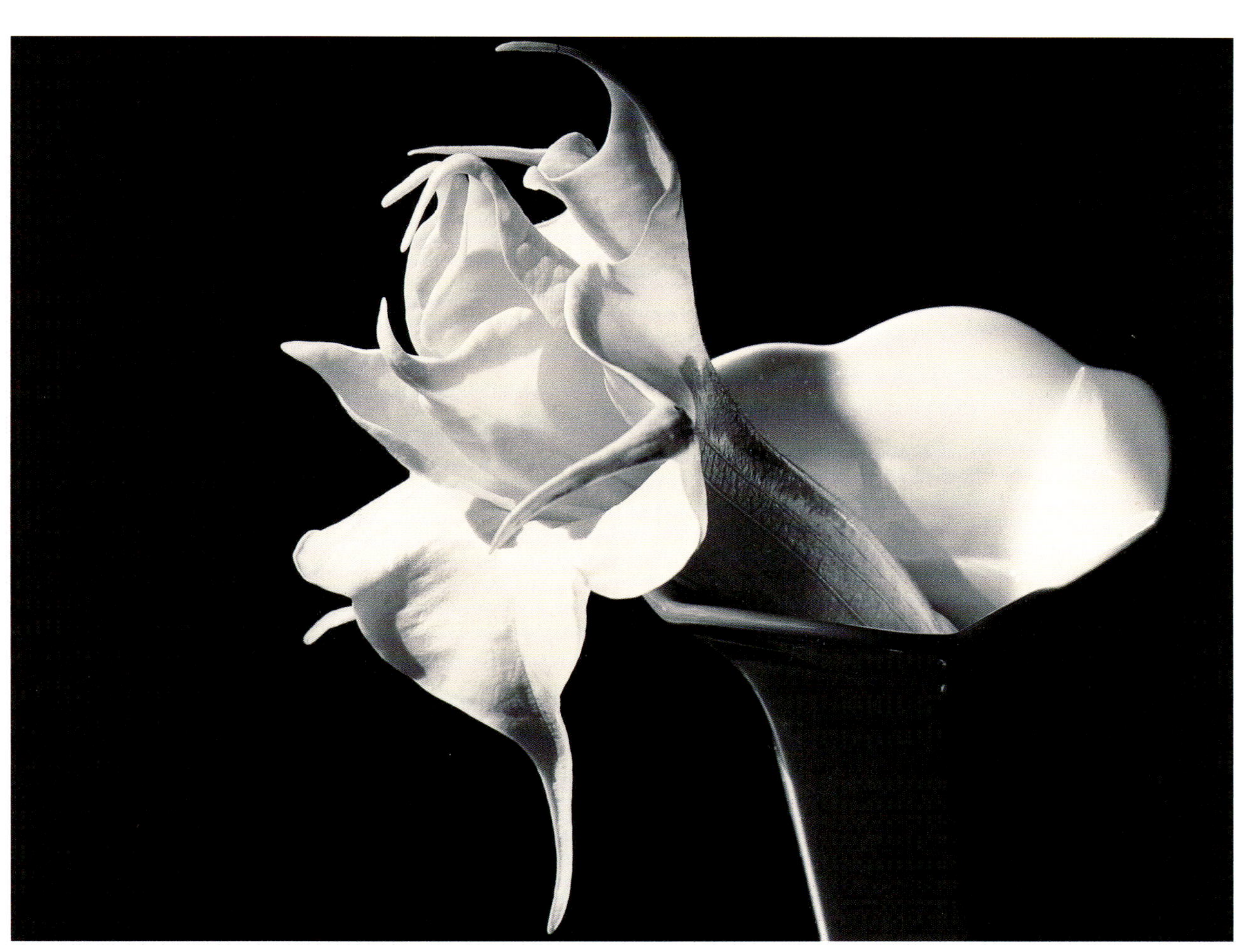

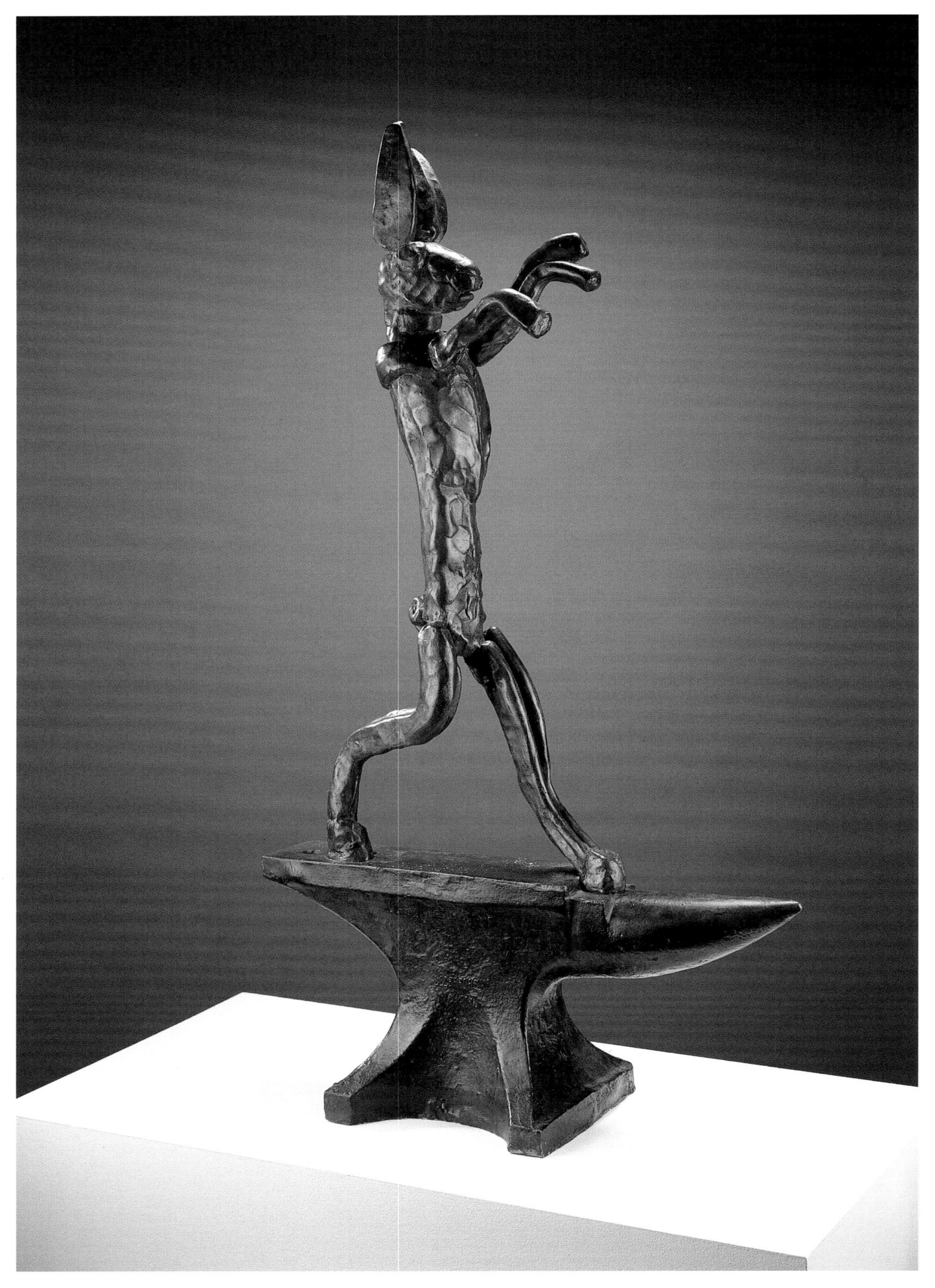

BARRY FLANAGAN

British, born 1941

Anvil (no belt), 1981, cast 1982

Bronze (edition 5/7 + 3)
40 × 23 × 9 inches
High Museum of Art, The Lenore and Burton Gold
   Collection of 20th-Century Art, 1999.105

From the beginning of his career, Barry Flanagan has opposed anything that he perceives as traditional. Something of an iconoclast by temperament, his deliberate flaunting of rules and expectations has helped the artist maintain a fresh approach in creating sculpture. Early on, he employed unorthodox materials like sand, cloth sacks, paper, and foam in ephemeral arrangements that challenged the notion of sculpture as something fixed, permanent, and rigid. As such practices became more widely accepted in the early 1970s, Flanagan turned to a durable medium with a long tradition: marble. By the end of the 1970s, his abstract works in stone gave way to bronze renderings of animals, including elephants, unicorns, and his now iconic hares, once again defying expectations. Relying on cultural associations of certain animal behaviors with human traits—for example, the wily hare or lumbering elephant—Flanagan's creatures portray the human condition.

The hare is a particularly apt surrogate for the human form—not quite as noble as the rest of the animal kingdom but still struggling with and against nature and somehow sympathetic in both its cunning and its foolishness. Sensually modeled in clay, then cast in bronze, Flanagan's hares are loosely rendered. The whimsy that pervaded Flanagan's earlier work becomes more immediately tangible in these sculptures. These are not cute bunnies, but they are extremely engaging. They are caught in a variety of energetic poses—leaping, dancing, and boxing—that highlight the hare's vitality and accentuate the vulnerability that comes with such high spirits. Lively and erratic according to legend, the hare has figured in everything from Aesop's *Fables* to Lewis Carroll's *Alice in Wonderland* to Richard Adams's *Watership Down.* In English, the hare is a metaphor for lunacy ("mad as a March hare," "a wild hare"), foolishness ("the hare and tortoise," "hare-brained"), or deceit ("run with the hare and the hounds").

The base for *Anvil (no belt)* offers a witty counterpoint to the pugnacious boxing hare atop it. The mass of the anvil provides ballast and stability to the lithe hare. This visual contrast also highlights the subtle shifts of meaning that Flanagan explores through his work. The blacksmith's anvil figuratively represents the weight of traditional craftsmanship, even as its function is reduced to a comical stage for the sinewy and slightly daft hare who appears ready to take on all comers.

Carrie Przybilla

DAN FLAVIN

American, 1933–1996

Untitled (To Donna), 1973
Blue, yellow, and pink fluorescent light tubes
(edition 2/5)
96 × 24 × 16½ inches
Collection of Burton Gold

In 1963, Dan Flavin mounted an ordinary fluorescent light tube diagonally on his studio wall, and with that simple act he began the work that he would expand upon, with surprising complexity, for more than thirty years. Flavin worked exclusively with the cheap, replaceable, and decidedly unglamorous medium of fluorescent light tubes. He used only the standard, factory-issued shapes (circular and straight) and colors (white, yellow, pink, blue, and green), with no embellishments or customization. His creative act was arranging the tubes.

Using such a strictly limited vocabulary of shapes and colors freed Flavin, in a sense, to explore the myriad ways in which they could be combined and arranged. He mounted fixtures horizontally, vertically, and diagonally, backward and forward, singly and in groups, and on the ceiling, wall, and floor. His compositions could be monochromatic or they could blend several colors of light for theatrical effects. *Untitled (To Donna)* consists of an eight-foot yellow fluorescent tube facing into a corner with two-foot blue and pink tubes facing out and bridging the corner at the top and bottom of the longer fixture. Flavin's structures often transform their architectural settings—the glow of this piece seems almost to make the corner dissolve.

Flavin's work is associated with the Minimalism of the late 1960s and early 1970s. Minimalism was cool, unemotional art, stripped down to regular, geometric elements that were industrially fabricated rather than handmade. It sought to remove any trace of the artist's hand, and in fact, anyone could replicate a Flavin identically with purchases from the local hardware store.

Unlike much Minimal art, however, Flavin's works are also charged with a great deal of emotion. Their glowing colors act as a sensual foil to the austerity of their composition; the light washes onto walls and floors, mixing there in beautiful and delicately nuanced pastel shades that would be impossible to duplicate with pigment. There is a mystery to these works that is at odds with the strictest Minimalism, for their emanating light gives them a presence, or aura, that extends far beyond their physical dimensions. One can detect a Flavin in the next room, even before rounding the corner to see it. They have an effect on everything around them.

There is also an inescapable element of spirituality in Flavin's work, although denied by the artist. Light has always been a metaphor for the divine; think of halos or the illumination of a cathedral through stained glass. However, the association of fluorescent lighting with particular places—stores, offices, schools, malls—will always, in the end, keep Flavin's work entrenched in our everyday, commercial world.

Anna Bloomfield

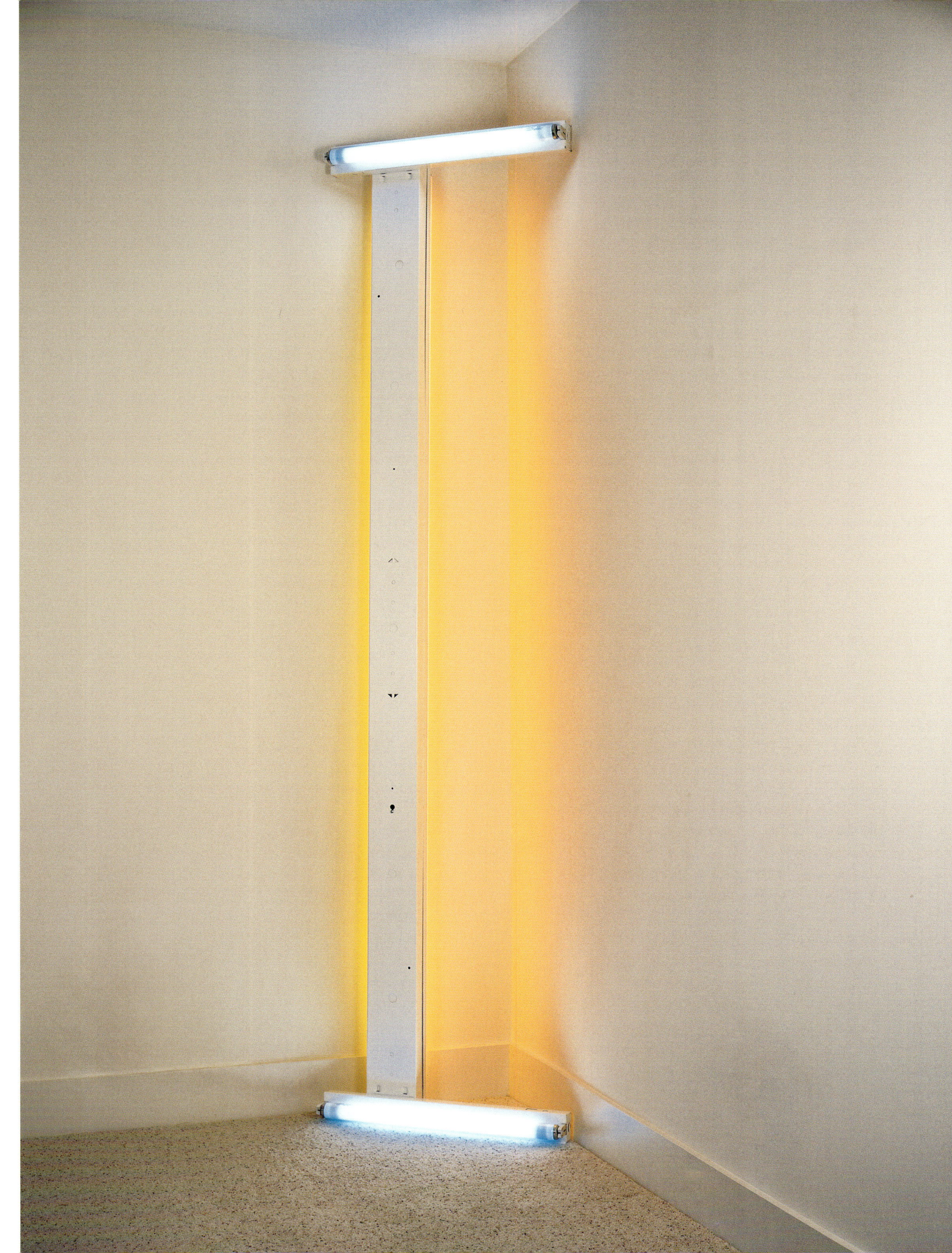

NANCY GRAVES

American, 1940–1996

Rope Pull, 1986

Iron, steel, bronze, polychromed patina, and
baked enamel
28 × 39 × 32 inches
High Museum of Art, The Lenore and Burton Gold
Collection of 20th-Century Art, 1999.107

As a child growing up in Pittsfield, Massa-
chusetts, Nancy Graves spent many hours at the
Berkshire Museum, which houses science, art, and
history displays side by side. This rich environment
fed her imagination and encouraged the nascent
artist to develop an appreciation for the beauty
of both dinosaur skeletons and Baroque sculpture. Throughout her career, Graves relied on
these early experiences, which helped her disre-
gard traditional distinctions between art and
science in the creation of her sculptures, paintings, films, drawings, and prints. Perhaps best
known for her lifelike sculptures of camels and
bones from the early 1970s, Graves looked to nature for her primary inspiration. She studied bio-
logical forms intently in order to understand their
fundamental physical structures, then added to
them her own aesthetic interpretations.

In 1979 Graves began to assemble an ever-
growing inventory of hundreds of exotic bronze
forms that she cast directly from such diverse
materials as seed pods, raffia fans, crayfish claws,
bananas, bubble wrap, machine parts, and farm
implements. Direct casting is an ancient technique
that retains delicate details from the original
form: an object is encased in clay and placed in
a kiln, which burns away the original but leaves
its impression. Molten metal—usually bronze—
is then poured into the ceramic shell, producing
a metal duplicate of the original object when the
shell is removed. Selecting from the rich variety
of shapes she thus preserved, Graves improvisa-
tionally assembled natural and man-made objects
into open structures, to which she then applied
patinas, paints, and enamels to create colors and
textures as diverse and visually active as her forms.

Rope Pull captures the whimsical charm typical
of Graves's mid-1980s work. The composition is
simultaneously abstract and representational—
strange forms seem suddenly to morph into recognizable objects, then dissolve into something
entirely different as the viewer's vantage point
changes. Every component, from pitchfork to
tropical flower, seems to balance on only one or
two points. The openwork basket tethered at the
top floats as if carried by a breeze, underscoring
the artist's perpetual desire to defy gravity. Areas
of pale green, sky blue, and deep orange accentuate this airy feeling and move the eye around
the composition, achieving an unexpected lyri-
cism and demonstrating that the whole is,
indeed, greater than the sum of its parts.

Carrie Przybilla

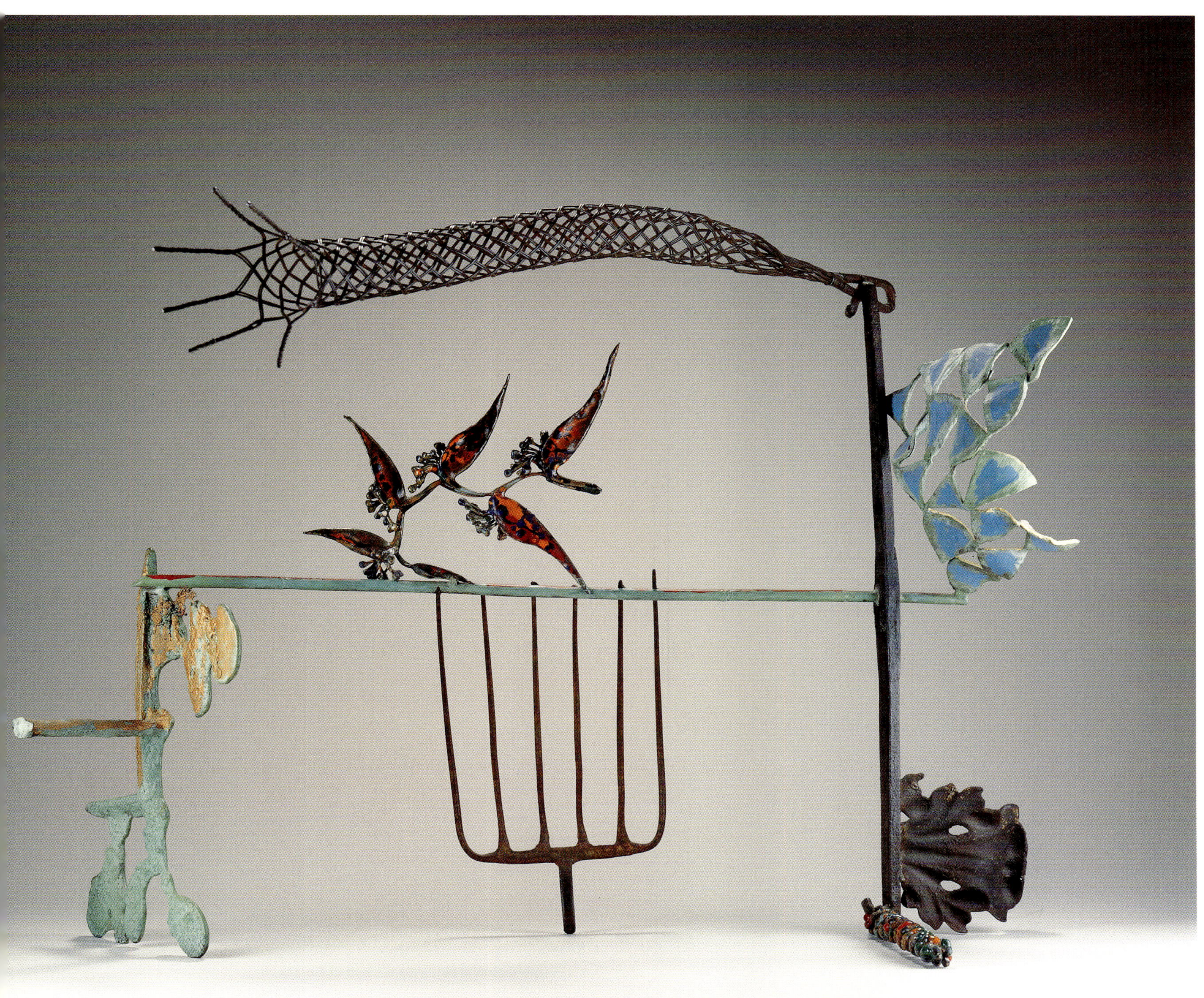

PETER HALLEY

American, born 1953

Gray to Black, 1988
Acrylic and Roll-a-Tex on canvas
65 × 135 × 3¼ inches
High Museum of Art, The Lenore and Burton Gold
  Collection of 20th-Century Art, 1999.108

As a painter, Peter Halley figures as a key
member of the so-called "neo-geo" movement of
the 1980s. A prolific writer, Halley has articulated
in his theoretical essays the concerns of artists
similarly exploring the relationship between modernist abstraction and postmodern consumer culture. This combination of roles has made him an
important voice for artists of his generation.

Halley's paintings depict labyrinths of lines and
squares that serve as metaphors for "the geom-
etrization of modern life."[1] His Day-Glo palette is
taken directly from popular culture and represents his interest in the intensity of contemporary
experience. The artist is intrigued by the ways in
which these vivid hues are used commercially to
attract attention (as in the packaging of products)
or to encode information (as with electrical wir-
ing). The thickly encrusted surfaces of his paintings result from Halley's use of Roll-a-Tex, an
artificial stucco commonly used in prefabricated
buildings. Like his vibrant colors, this texture refers to consumer culture and connects his work
to the concerns of the Pop artists of the 1960s,
just as the crisp lines and spare forms in his paintings reflect Halley's interest in the cool, analytical
reductive style of Minimalism.

The artist deliberately straddles the line between abstraction and representation, saying, "I
don't think of my work as abstract at all; instead of
using the word abstract I always use the word dia-
grammatic."[2] His rectilinear compositions serve as
symbolic diagrams of the vast technological and
communication networks that undergird modern
existence. Halley explains that he is "interested in
the two-dimensional, graphic quality of contemporary life; flat information—architectural diagrams,
corporate flow charts, electronic circuit boards—
have come to dominate our cognitive universe."[3]

Halley's terminology underscores his belief.
He uses the word "cell" to describe the large
central square that has appeared in most of his
paintings since 1982. Originally conceived of as a
prison, the form of the cell embodies the idealis-
tic formalism of high modernism, while the term
can take on a variety of meanings, many linked
to technology. "Conduit" identifies the lines that
emerge from Halley's cells, often connecting them
to one another, and, like "cell," the term "conduit" has many associations, particularly with
electrical circuitry. The conduits unify his compositions, which are always multipaneled and usually

divided horizontally into a thin lower canvas,
through which most of the conduits run, abutted
by a large upper canvas that contains a cell. Like
his terminology, Halley's formal decisions are
multivalent metaphors: the division of his compositions among panels can be read simultaneously
as a diagram of what is above and below ground,
a boundary between the visible and invisible, and
the separation of the conscious and subconscious
mind. In addition to providing formal unity, the
conduits connect these oppositions and compound
their psychological resonance.

Gray to Black is somewhat atypical in that it

does not contain one of Halley's signature cells. The artist has maintained his usual division of above and below, however: a large expanse of black rests atop a long, narrow horizontal panel containing two blazing orange conduits. Their glow implies a two-way transmission of energy or data, although source and destination are unclear. Halley's title, usually a straightforward description of the composition, here seems confusing, because the eye sees only black and orange. Slowly, however, the gray, almost imperceptibly lighter than the black, shows itself on the left, revealing that the composition is a triptych.

Although the distinction is visually subtle, the conceptual ramifications imply a potential for disruption that belies the controlled order of the composition.

Carrie Przybilla

1. Halley, quoted in Eleanor Heartney, "Simulationism, The Hot New Cool Art," *ARTnews* 87, no. 1 (January 1987), p. 134.
2. Quoted in Jeanne Siegel, "The Artist/Critic of the 80s: Peter Halley," in *Artwords 2: Discourse on the Early 80s*, ed. Jeanne Siegel (Ann Arbor/London: UMI Research Press, 1988), p. 235.
3. Quoted in Kristine McKenna, "Halley's New Universe: Spirituality and Technology," *Los Angeles Times*, 14 December 1990, sec. F, p. 23, col. 1.

ANN HAMILTON

American, born 1956

Untitled (Stone Book), 1992

Book, stones, lacquered birch, and glass
3⅝ × 38⅝ × 9¼ inches
Collection of Burton Gold

I long to get hold of language, and deal with words the way I can deal with materials.

—Ann Hamilton[1]

The immense and the infinitesimal coexist in Ann Hamilton's installations. Improbable materials such as honey, horsehair, and face powder have become hallmarks of her work. Her wondrous environments, which have filled whole buildings, frequently incorporate a solitary "attendant" who performs simple repetitive tasks, like folding shirts. Since the late 1980s, the artist has infused her work with language in a variety of forms: a video of a mouth trying to speak despite being filled with stones; a floor made of printers' type; enormous Braille letters embossed on the walls of a room. Her ultimate purpose is to probe the nature of expectations, the relationship of language to knowledge, and art's ability to embody the ineffable.

In 1992 Hamilton created the first in a series of installations in which attendants methodically obliterated the texts from books by erasing, burning, or cutting. That same year, the New Museum of Contemporary Art in New York commissioned her to produce a limited-edition book sold to benefit the museum. For this untitled project she selected a total of fifty-four old books (forty in the edition plus fourteen artist's proofs) based on their physical characteristics—size, wear, and paper quality—and typographic layout. The artist opened each book to its middle, excised six or eight pages, and reattached them, edge to edge, to the right-hand side of the opened page spread to make an accordion-fold extension from the book. She then rendered the texts illegible by meticulously gluing tiny stones over every visible letter. Finally, Hamilton encased each book in a shallow vitrine whose width equaled the span of her outstretched arms. The neat rows of pebbles—nestled in blocks matching the proportions of the columns of text beneath them—form a miniature landscape, a rugged, multicolored terrain that offers a seductive alternative to language. The desire to read is confounded by the voluptuous materiality of the book, even as the pure sensual pleasure of looking at it is disrupted by the mystery of the obliterated text.

Like much of Hamilton's work, this book serves as a critique of contemporary rhetoric that tries to locate power in naming or knowledge in accumulated words. The clearly obsessive labor involved in obscuring the book's text dissolves meaning into a series of ephemeral moments, each nearly identical to the ones before and after it. Each stone reminds us that language is a system of communication, not knowledge in its own right, and that words are just another form of representation, abstract symbols for objects, actions, and ideas. Hamilton replaces words on a page with textures and colors that can be experienced and understood directly, without representation. In so doing, the artist advocates a kind of knowing that lies beyond words. "Ultimately," she says of her work, "it's its own poem; you can't approach it with language."[2]

Carrie Przybilla

1. Hamilton, "a conversation with ann hamilton," interview by Hugh M. Davies and Lynda Forsha, in *ann hamilton,* ed. Lynda Forsha (San Diego: San Diego Museum of Contemporary Art, 1991), p. 71.
2. Ibid., p. 62.

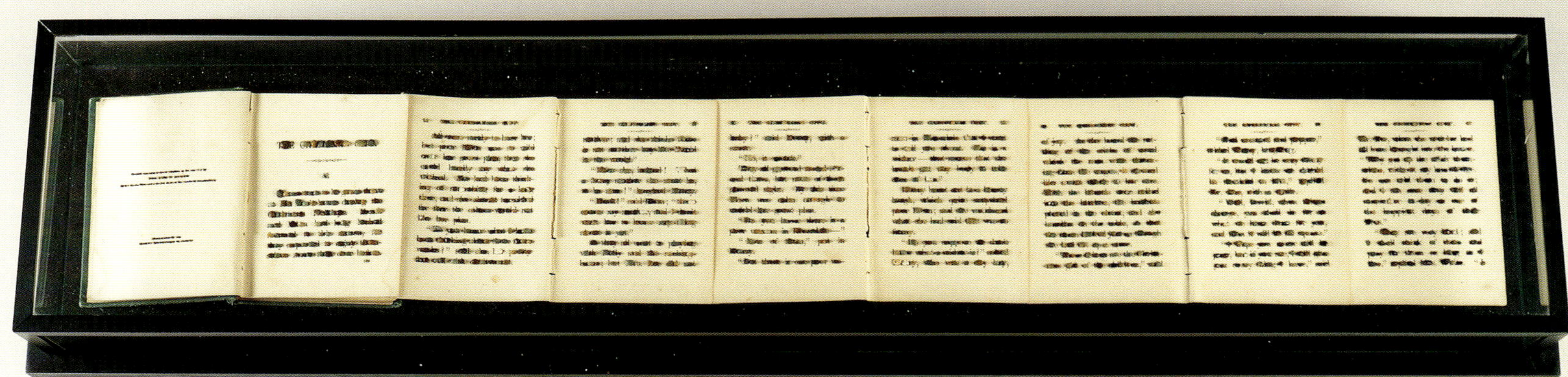

13

JENNY HOLZER

American, born 1950

Untitled, from the "Living" series, 1989
Bethel white granite (edition 2/3)
27½ × 36 × 18 inches
High Museum of Art, The Lenore and Burton Gold
 Collection of 20th-Century Art, 1999.113

Originally trained as a painter, Jenny Holzer is a product of the TV age and the world of advertising and billboards. She borrows freely from mass culture as she examines contemporary issues and raises questions about the nature of originality and the value of the artist's hand in the making of art. Her works mimic common formats, such as handbills and LED signs, that imply impersonal messages. She contrasts these forms with texts that range from simple one-liners to enigmatic elegies and meditations on the human condition that seem by turns thoughtful, humorous, and sincere. Holzer's work is often subversive: her messages and their formats challenge our assumptions about art and its role in society today. Lean and elegant in appearance, Holzer's work is a complex amalgam of conceptual premise, Pop imagery, and ironic interchange between object and void, presence and absence, desire and loss.

Holzer first gained attention in 1978 with a series of posters with lists of pithy, often contradictory slogans that began to appear anonymously around Manhattan. These works, part of her "Truisms" series, were inspired by a reading list that was part of the Whitney Museum's Independent Study Program when the artist was enrolled in the course in 1977. The list included studies in art and literature, Marx, psychology, social and cultural theory, criticism, and feminism, which she attempted to summarize and satirize in a series of mock clichés, such as "Abuse of power comes as no surprise" and "Protect me from what I want."

This untitled work from 1989 takes the form of a granite bench. The text incised on it comes from a series of writings Holzer began in 1980, immediately following the "Truisms" series:

MORE THAN ONCE I'VE AWAKENED WITH

TEARS RUNNING DOWN MY CHEEKS

I HAVE HAD TO THINK WHETHER

I WAS CRYING OR WHETHER IT

WAS INVOLUNTARY LIKE DROOLING

Called the "Living" series, these texts take a subjective tone as they reflect and comment on personal concerns. They originally appeared as a series of bronze wall plaques but, like many of her other texts, have migrated into a variety of media. Over the years, Holzer's writing has continued to become more subjective as she has abandoned the role of a seemingly neutral, anonymous observer and adopted voices that reflect private thoughts and emotions. Her work continues to take familiar forms, however, continually surprising viewers with unexpected messages in deceptively innocuous formats.

Carrie Przybilla

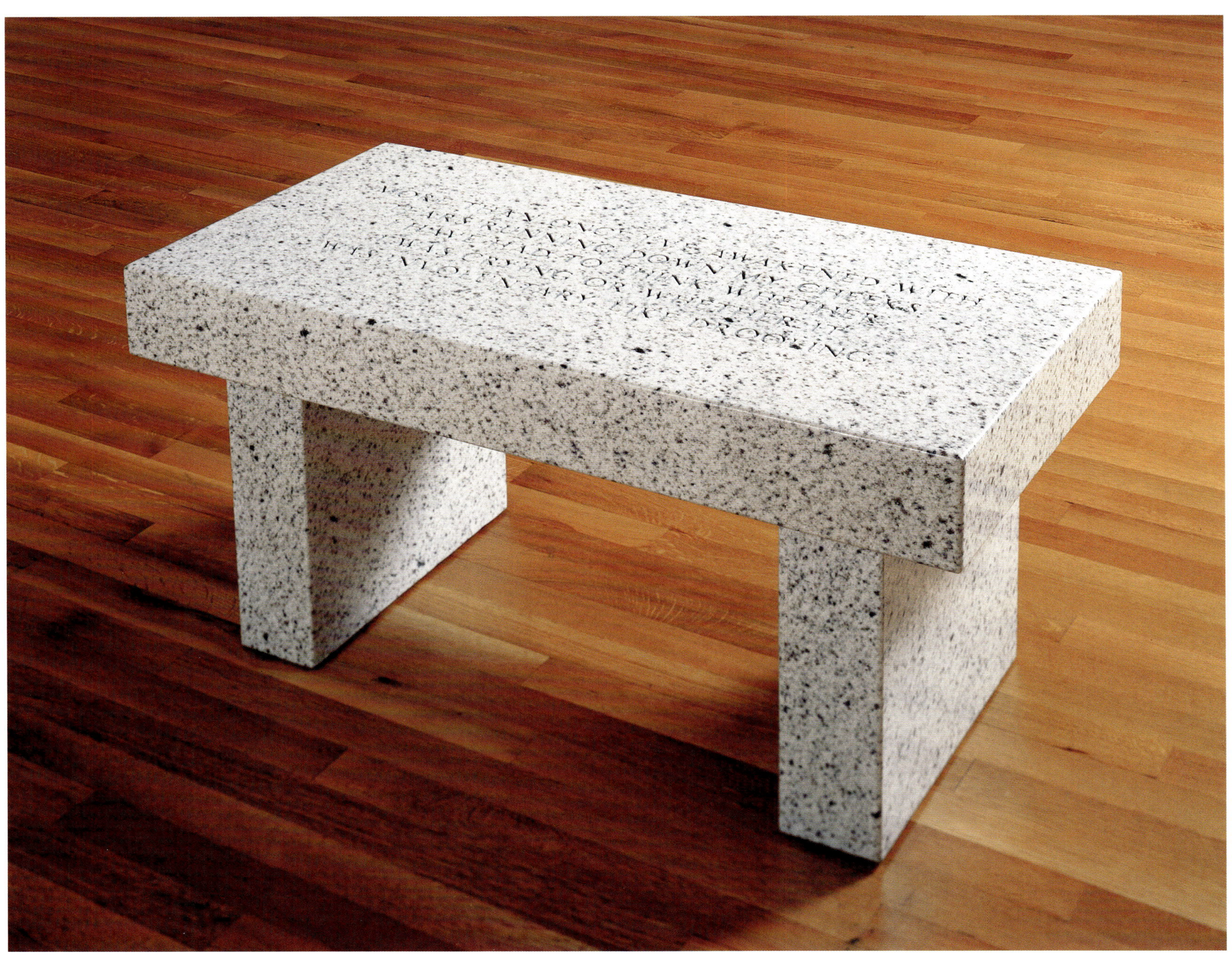
MORE THAN ONCE I'VE AWAKENED WITH
TEARS RUNNING DOWN MY CHEEKS.
I HAVE HAD TO THINK WHETHER
IT WAS CRYING OR WHETHER IT
WAS INVOLUNTARY, LIKE DROOLING.

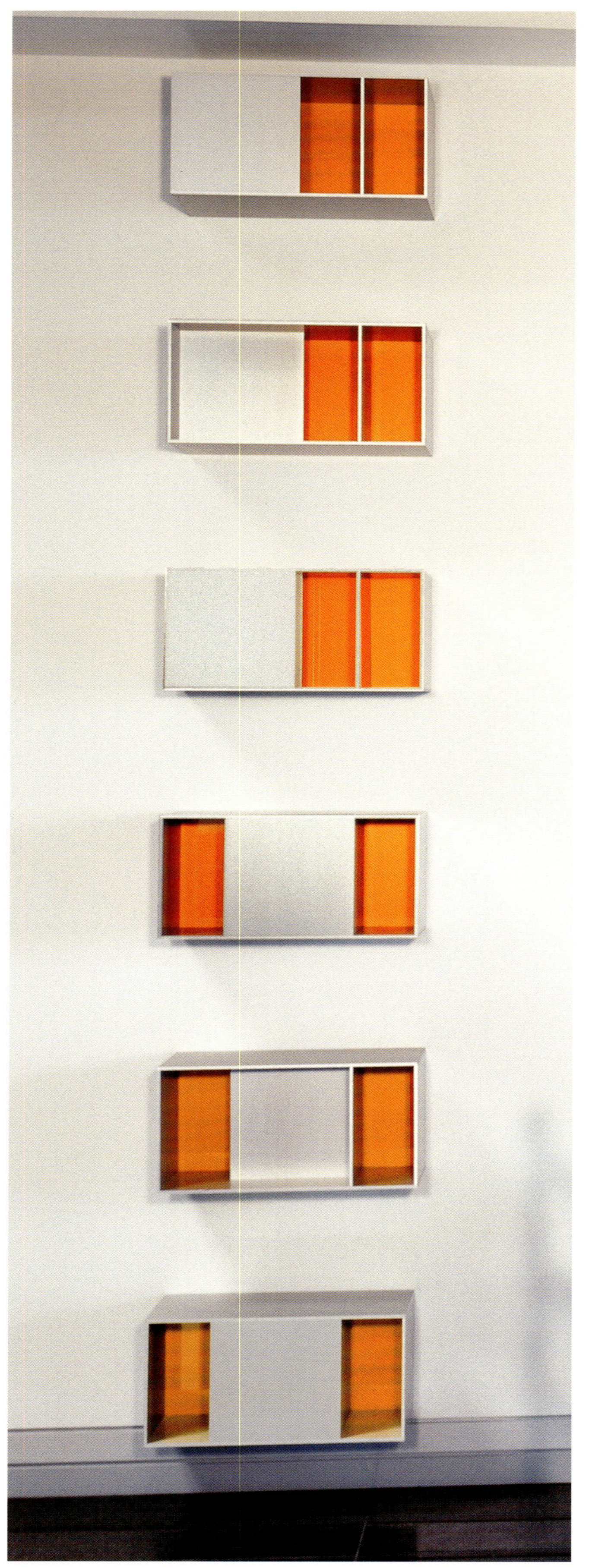

14

DONALD JUDD

American, 1928–1994

Untitled, 1988

Aluminum and Plexiglas
Six elements, each 9⅞ × 19¾ × 9⅞ inches;
   overall installed: 119¼ × 19¾ × 9⅞ inches
Promised gift of Burton Gold to the High Museum of
   Art for The Lenore and Burton Gold Collection of
   20th-Century Art

Donald Judd's art epitomizes Minimalism.
His reductive, geometric sculptures exemplify the
modernist urge to purify form and media that
came to full fruition in the 1960s. Something of
a prodigy, Judd began private art lessons while
still a child. He continued to study art through
college, even while he pursued a degree in philosophy, graduating *cum laude* in 1953 from
Columbia University. He returned to Columbia in
1957 as a graduate student in art history; by 1959
he was regularly writing reviews for *Arts* magazine, all the while continuing his own artistic
practice. As a critic, his commanding, unequivocal
views clearly articulated the framework in which
his art and that of his peers was discussed. His
work, as both an artist and a critic, forced a re-
evaluation of the intent and expressive potential
of sculpture.

Judd opposed all forms of illusionism and
expressionism. He rejected any device (other than
the object itself) that might be seen as representational or symbolic, or that might deter the
direct ordering of the viewer's perception. He
strove to concretize sensation, to make it immediate rather than a consequence of interpreting an
image or metaphor. In Judd's work, structure and
image are identical. He stripped sculpture to its
bare essence, constructing his work from simple
geometric forms arranged according to a prede-
termined serial repetition or arithmetic progres-
sion. As a result, a sense of order pervades his art,
even though its parameters may be difficult to
define. Just as he advocated directness and simplicity in form, Judd favored the use of industrial
materials, particularly metal and plastic. The result

is always straightforward. The materials are
only minimally manipulated, so his surfaces are
smooth and nontactile, bearing no evidence of
the artist's hand. Different materials delineate
the various components of each sculpture. Because he frequently used materials as they came
from the factory, a change of material often also
entails a change of color. Thus material, color,
and surface are identical, avoiding any possibility
of illusion.

The cool rationality of Judd's work is readily
apparent in this wall-mounted sculpture from
1988. Six rectangular aluminum boxes are
mounted vertically, one above another, with
equal space between them. Each box has two
openings of equal size in the front, through which
one can see the yellow Plexiglas that forms the
back of the box. In the top three boxes, the openings adjoin one another on the right half of the
box. In the lower three boxes, the openings are
at opposite ends. The combined size of the openings equals half the front surface, the other half
of which is covered by a square of aluminum that
is alternately flush with the surface of the box or
slightly recessed. At first glance, the boxes appear
almost as a single entity, and certainly identical.
As the differences reveal themselves, however,
the discovery of each deviation makes the eye
acutely aware of ever more subtle variations. At
the same time, one almost instinctively recognizes
an emerging pattern, which serves to unify the
disparate parts of the composition.

Carrie Przybilla

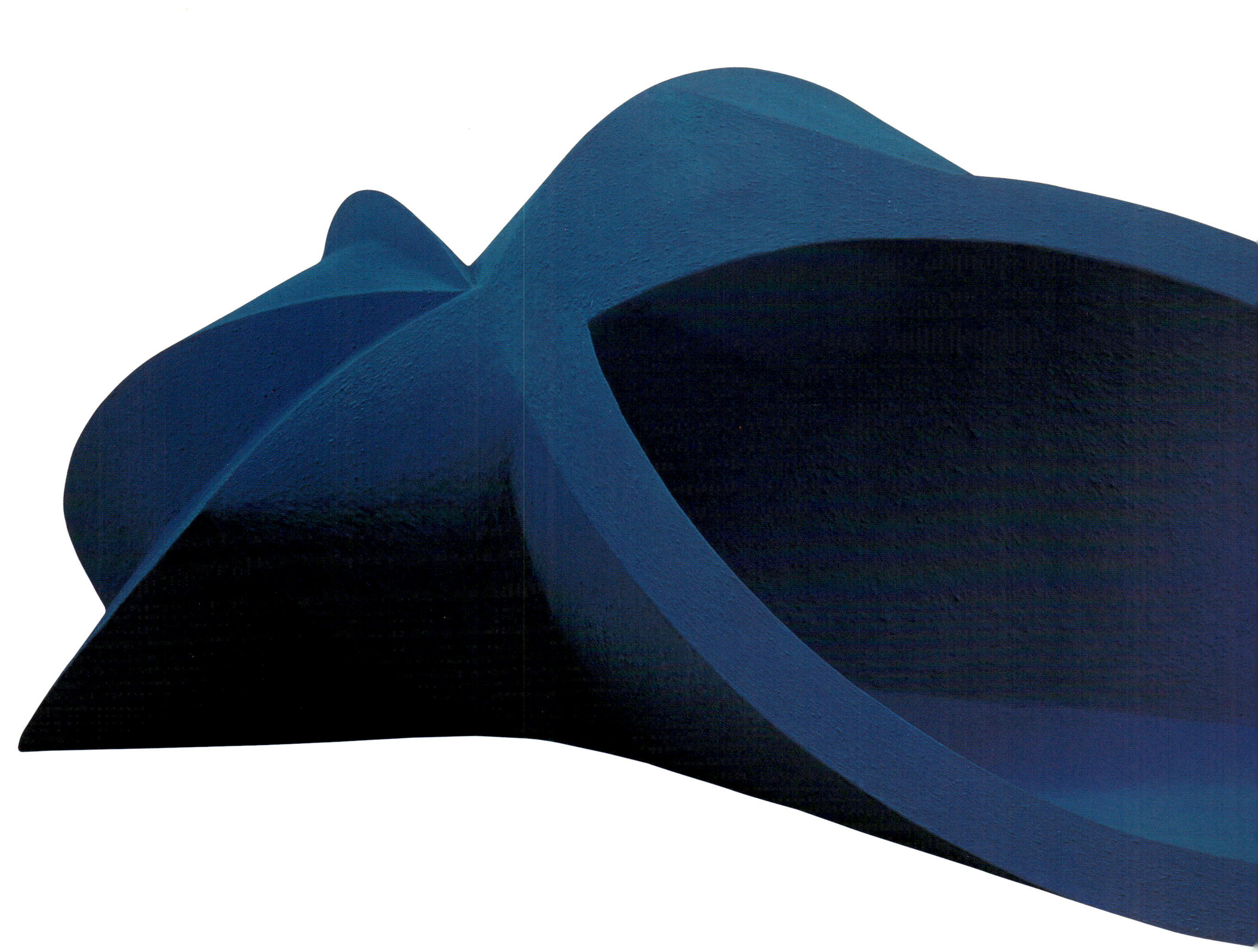

ANISH KAPOOR

British, born India, 1954

Pot for Her, 1985
Wood, gesso, and pigment
38 × 96 × 42 inches
High Museum of Art, The Lenore and Burton Gold
   Collection of 20th-Century Art, 1999.104

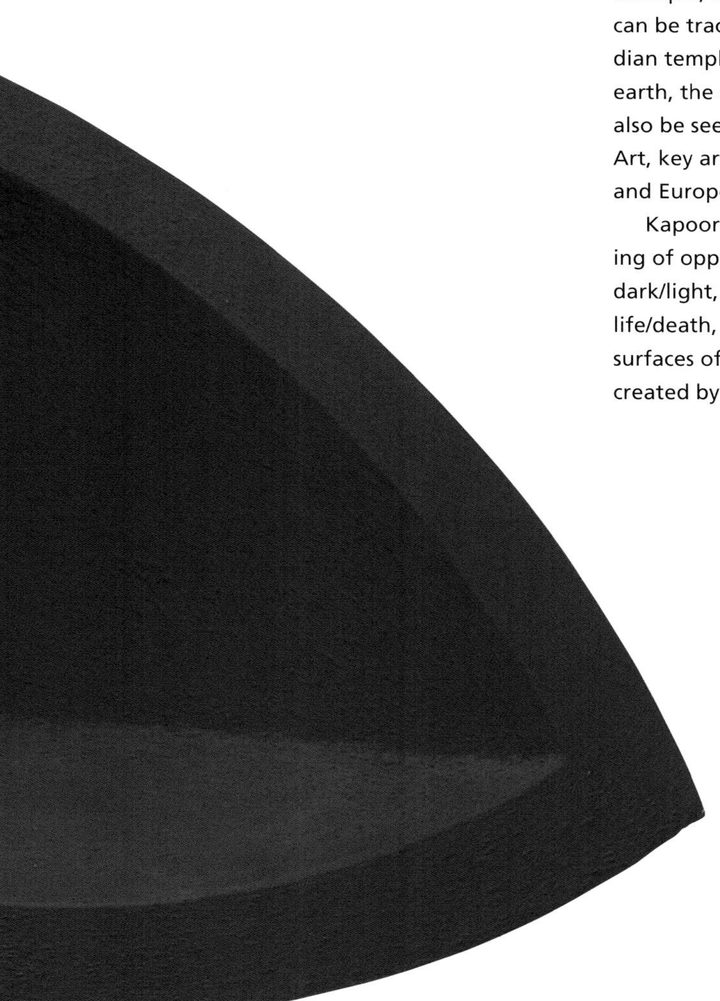

Let's think of the first person who made a pot. I feel it was almost certainly a woman. Let us say that she went to the riverside and found a lump of clay and was able, with a few subtle movements of her hands, to transform it into a pot. What has happened is that the clay is completely changed. It is now a pot. It has a new function, a new purpose and—what's most important—a new name. The ability to give a new name is, in a way, this act of transformation.

—Anish Kapoor[1]

The son of a Hindu father and Jewish mother, Anish Kapoor was born in Bombay, raised in Delhi, and attended art school in London. Not surprisingly, given his rich cultural background, he dislikes designations of nationality, regarding them as limiting. Both Western and Eastern traditions inform his lyrical abstract sculptures. For example, his signature use of powdered pigments can be traced to rituals he saw performed in Indian temples that celebrate the fecundity of the earth, the source of all life. These pigments can also be seen as related to *arte povera* and Earth Art, key artistic movements in the United States and Europe in the 1960s and 1970s.

Kapoor's work typically incorporates a melding of opposites: surface/volume, interior/exterior, dark/light, male/female, conscious/unconscious, life/death, spirit/matter. The powdered-pigment surfaces of his sculptures exemplify the tension created by such dualities: their velvety texture invites the viewer to touch, although to do so would spoil the fragile surface. As a result, the viewer experiences a suspended state of longing and desire. The sensuality of Kapoor's colors and surfaces underscores the sexual allusions in his forms. At the same time, there is an ethereal quality to his work that clearly seeks to rise above mere physicality. The artist emphasizes, "I wish to make sculpture about belief, or about passion, about experience that is outside of material concern."[2] Although there are personal elements in his work, Kapoor's goal is to reveal the sublime: "I think it's my role as an artist to bring to expression, it's not my role to be expressive. I've got nothing particular to say, I don't have any message to give anyone. But it is my role to bring to expression, let's say, to divine means that allow phenomenological and other perceptions which one might use, one might work with, and then move towards a poetic existence."[3] To do this, he tries to "provide a place of quietness, of singularity . . . with the hope that if one can slow the world down enough, make the act of looking particular enough, everything that needs to happen in terms of remembrance will happen."[4]

Pot for Her beautifully demonstrates the dualities and transformation characteristic of Kapoor's art. Rendered in rich blue, a hue the artist associates with the divine, the recumbent form is simultaneously figurative and abstract, phallic and vaginal, organic and geometric. The work's swelling middle, like its title, implies that it is some sort of vessel. The contents remain hidden, however, taking on a mystery that transcends this exquisite shell.

Carrie Przybilla

1. Quoted in Marco Livingstone, *Anish Kapoor: Feeling into Form* (Lyon, France: Le Nouveau Musée, 1983), p. 27.
2. Quoted in Michael Newman, *Objects and Figures: New Sculpture in Britain* (Edinburgh, Scotland: Fruitmarket Gallery, 1982), unpaginated.
3. Quoted in "Anish Kapoor: The colour issue," *The Observer* (London), 12 April 1998, Life Page, p. 4.
4. Quoted in Homi K. Bhabha, "Anish Kapoor: Making Emptiness," in Homi K. Bhabha and Pier Luigi Tazzi, *Anish Kapoor* (London: Hayward Gallery; Berkeley: University of California Press, 1998), p. 11.

ALEX KATZ

American, born 1927

Blue Umbrella #2, 1972
Lithograph (edition 67/120)
20⅛ × 30 inches
High Museum of Art, The Lenore and Burton Gold
    Collection of 20th-Century Art, given in memory
    of Elisa Hydee Levine, 1982.52

Alex Katz's work is frequently identified
as part of the Pop Art movement of the 1960s.
Certainly, he is of the same generation as Andy
Warhol and Roy Lichtenstein, and the stylized
simplification of his figures seems to signal a similar approach to representational painting. Katz's
work, however, lacks the ironic interest in popular
culture characteristic of Pop Art. Since the late
1950s, his favorite subjects have been his friends
and family depicted in mundane settings. The
artist's combination of photorealism with a deliberate naïveté makes these ordinary scenes somehow compelling, eliciting unexpected poetry
from an apparently mechanized style.

Despite the ascendance of Abstract Expressionism in the early 1950s, when Katz was coming
of age artistically, he chose to pursue objective
painting and made it look contemporary by
exploring the border between abstraction and
representation. From the beginning, he has emphasized the flatness of the picture plane by pre-
senting his subjects in close-up views, simplifying
forms, and applying color in uninflected fields.
Although his work looks easy, it's actually the
result of a lengthy process that begins with live
models and involves preliminary drawings, oil
sketches, and cutouts. The artist synthesizes these
studies into a large drawing that is then traced
onto the canvas. Because traditional signs of
depth or solidity are flattened by his application
of color, shifts from reading surface to reading
depth are abrupt, focusing attention back to the
process of the picture's making. Katz's work sits

at that delicate point where representation is
specific enough to evoke real individuals yet
general enough to prevent viewers from being
seduced by the detail of realist painting. He presents a level of visual information similar to that
found in cartooning or caricature, but scrupu-
lously avoids both.

Although Katz has repeatedly used certain
models over the years, his favorite, by far, is his
wife Ada. One gets no sense of their personal
relationship from his depictions of her, however.
He is basically interested in people as types, their
individual characteristics subordinated to the
overall composition. Although his canvases often
deal with figures in a specific setting, the artist
eschews narrative or psychological meaning. His
handling of paint is not expressionistic, and he
avoids most other signs of overt emotion. In
general, his figures hardly seem to communicate
at all. Thus, *Blue Umbrella #2* is typical of Katz's
oeuvre. The composition of this print is nearly
identical to an eponymous oil painting from the
same year. Both show a woman—Ada—wearing
a raincoat and carrying an umbrella. She could be
anyone passing on the street during a busy rush
hour, that stranger seen briefly whose face lingers
in the mind's eye. Despite the intensive labor of
his working process, Katz captures the momentary quality of this encounter and evokes the pe-
culiar selectivity of memory.

Carrie Przybilla

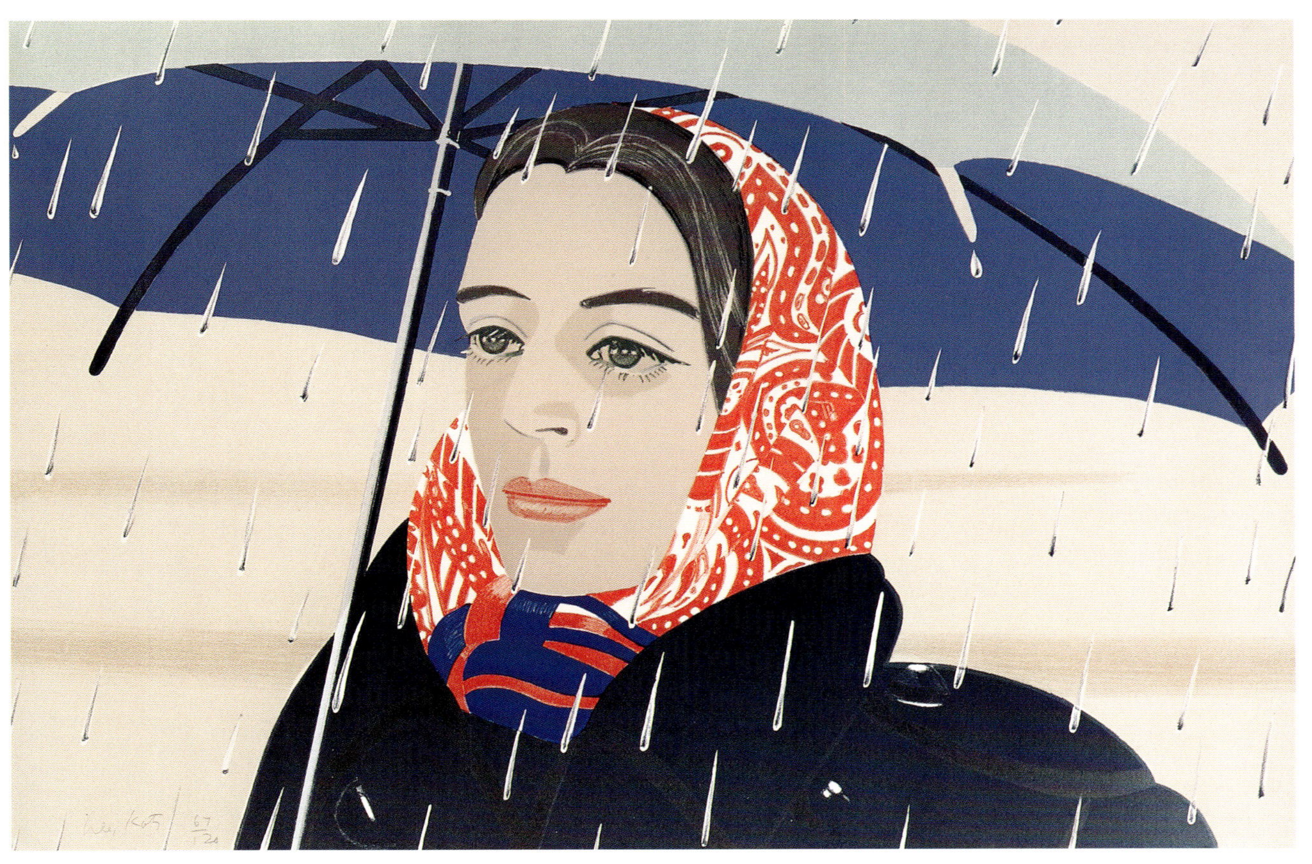

17

MEL KENDRICK

American, born 1949

Large Poplar with Holes and Grooves, 1985
Poplar
49½ × 27½ × 20 inches
Collection of Burton Gold

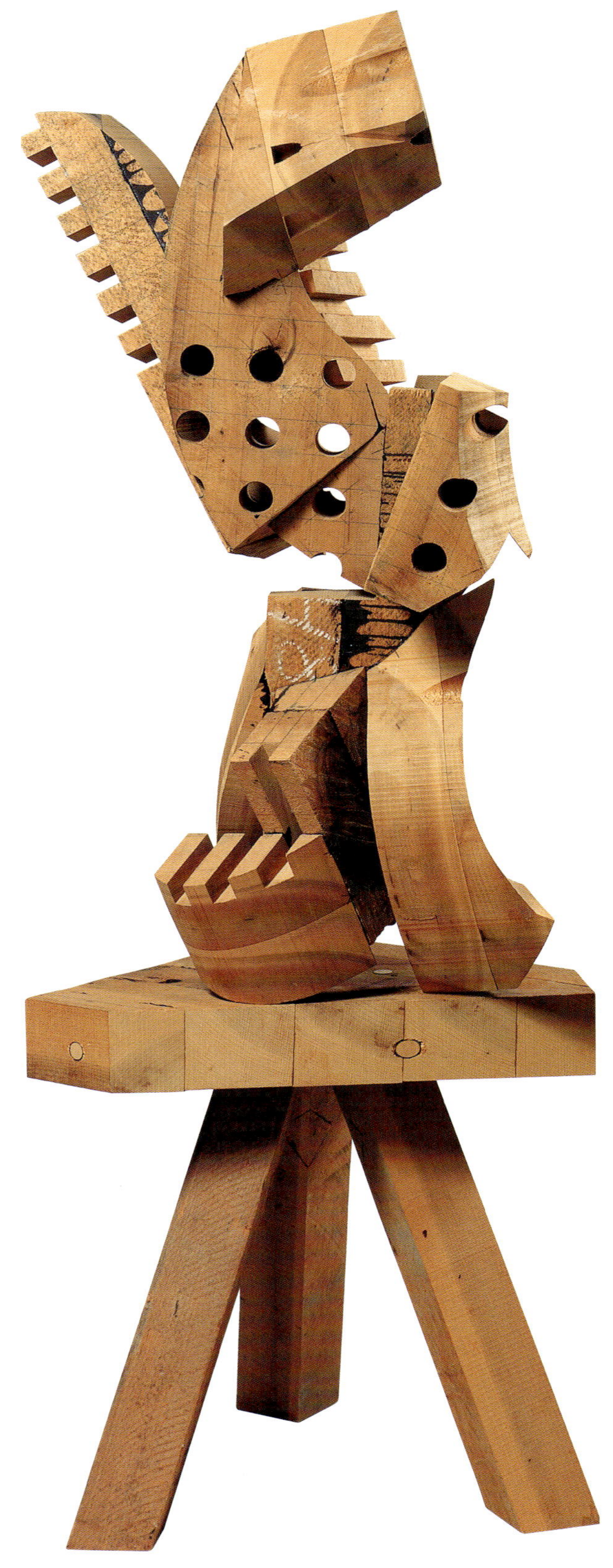

Mel Kendrick is one of a generation of sculp-tors who established their reputations after the 1970s, when the severe geometry, cool industrial materials, and imposing scale of Minimalism had dominated sculpture. At the beginning of his career Kendrick worked in this prevailing style, but in the early 1980s he made an abrupt shift and began crafting small, handworked sculptures in wood. This change was the result of the artist's realization that "scale doesn't matter, a work doesn't have to be big to be good. Sculpture doesn't have to be a massive, physical thing. My small pieces . . . were far more direct, far more enjoyable to make, and, I realized, far more personal."[1] This piece, *Large Poplar with Holes and Grooves,* is about four feet tall—larger than many of Kendrick's most intimate works of the early 1980s, but still far from monumental in scale.

Kendrick creates each sculpture from a single block of wood, which he first cuts up with a chain saw. He may then drill, chisel, or groove the wood—creating flowing curves, sharp angles, and rhythmically repeated ridges—before rearranging the parts into a new whole. "It's not a challenge to use the whole block," he says. "It's just a way of working. It gives the pieces an internal logic that is not necessarily retrievable—but whatever I've done to the piece you can sense it. Somehow this part relates to this other part, though you don't have to go around trying to match it up or figuring out how it happened."[2] Lines drawn on the block to guide the cutting often remain visible on the finished work, as do drips of glue and the wooden dowels used to join the elements. In this way, each sculpture carries a record of the process and history of its making.

Kendrick's working method is spontaneous and intuitive. As he has described it, "It's not usually until the very end of the process that the sculpture has a top or a bottom. Frequently the sculptures grow from the center like crystals. Recently my tendency has been to draw less on the wood and to work directly with the saw."[3]

Kendrick usually makes bases for his sculptures, often out of the same sort of wood as the work—in this case, poplar. This practice runs counter to Minimalism's insistence that bases be eliminated and sculptures be placed directly on the floor or wall in order to emphasize their continuity with the real world. Kendrick's return to the pedestal, however, seems to have a mostly practical intent. As he says, "I use a base because I want my work to be seen at eye level and to engage the viewer."[4]

Anna Bloomfield

1. Quoted in Michael Boodro, "Mel Kendrick: Calculated Risks," *ARTnews* 90, no. 5 (May 1991), p. 108.
2. Kendrick, "Talking Objects: Interviews with Ten Younger Sculptors," interview by Wade Saunders, *Art in America* 73, no. 11 (November 1985), p. 123.
3. Quoted in Betsy Siersma, *Mel Kendrick Recent Sculpture* (Amherst: University of Massachusetts at Amherst, 1986), p. 20.
4. Quoted in ibid., p. 22.

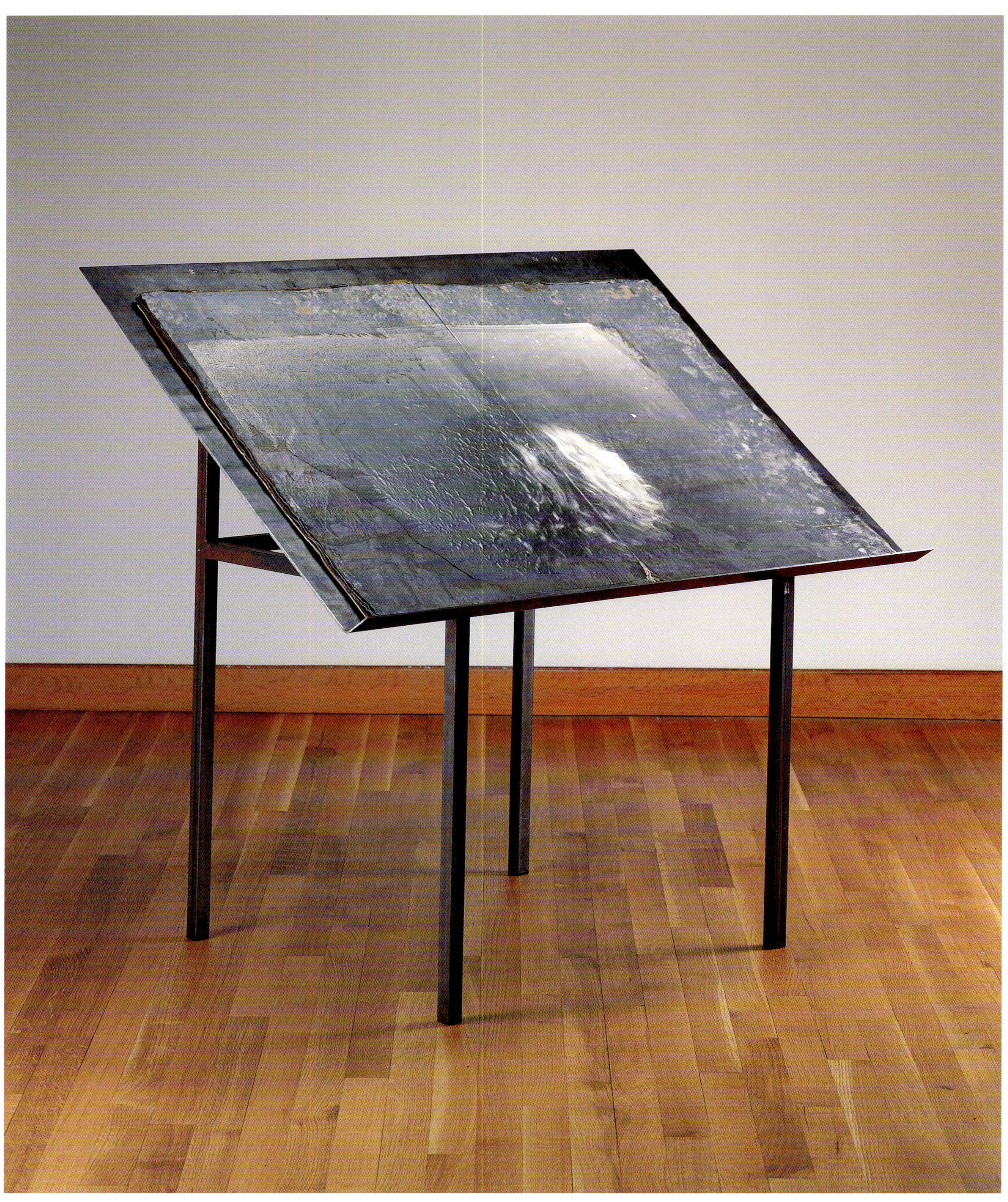

ANSELM KIEFER

German, born 1945

Brunhilde Sleeps, 1987

Book with eight double lead pages with clay, acrylic, and photographs, mounted on board with canvas, and steel stand
Book (closed): 28 × 19¾ × 2 inches; stand: 40½ × 43¼ × 26¾ inches
High Museum of Art, The Lenore and Burton Gold Collection of 20th-Century Art, 1996.5

An interest in history comes naturally to Anselm Kiefer. He was born just months before the end of World War II and raised in the Black Forest region near the east bank of the Rhine. His father, a teacher of art and art history, named him after the nineteenth-century classical painter Anselm Feuerbach. As a student of Joseph Beuys's in the early 1970s, he developed a love of ancient myths and a belief that these sagas are part of a collective consciousness. In his books, paintings, and installations, Kiefer invokes the Germanic influence on history and culture in order to remind viewers that these often-admirable contributions to civilization also set the stage for the barbarism of World War II. His art turns subjects the Nazis rendered unspeakable into reflections on contemporary life. For Kiefer, "art is the only possibility of making a connection between disparate things and thus creating a meaning. . . . I see history as synchronous, whether it's the Sumerians with their epic of Gilgamesh or German mythology. As far as I am concerned the old sagas are not old at all, nor is the Bible. When you go to them, most things are already formulated."[1]

Since he was an art student, Kiefer has frequently used Siegfried and Brunhilde, key characters in the *Nibelungenlied,*[2] in his art. He has known their story since childhood: a thirteenth-century manuscript kept in his hometown is thought to be the oldest and most complete German rendition of the epic tale. Richard Wagner's opera cycle, *The Ring of the Nibelungen,* is prob-

ably the most familiar retelling. The Wagnerian version, in particular, makes postwar Germans nervous because it is remembered as a favorite of the Nazis. The tale revolves around a ring made from gold stolen from a magical cache deep beneath the Rhine River. Wotan, king of the gods, covets the ring, even though it is cursed and will bring destruction to anyone who wears it. When his daughter Brunhilde, a divine Valkyrie, thwarts his attempt to possess it, Wotan casts her into a deep sleep. Siegfried, the naïve young hero, slays the dragon that guards the ring and takes it as his own. A short time later he comes upon the sleeping Brunhilde and awakens her. They immediately fall in love and pledge themselves to one another. To honor her vow, Brunhilde willingly sacrifices her immortality. Siegfried, however, falls victim to a passion for adventure and is tricked into taking a potion that causes him to forget his vows. He regains his memory and realizes his error only as he lies dying. With his last breath, he once again declares his love for Brunhilde, who realizes that he was duped. She throws the accursed ring back into the Rhine, then rides into Siegfried's funeral pyre, the flames of which engulf both heaven and earth.

Through the figure of Brunhilde, Kiefer reflects on the nature of love. From the beginning of the story, when the gold is stolen, a dichotomy is established. The women in the story, who prize love above all, symbolize goodness and purity. The men, however, are willing to sacrifice love if

it interferes with their ambition. Only Brunhilde is courageous, honorable, and wise. She alone sees the truth, experiences love and compassion, and turns her back on greed and power by returning the ring. The story demonstrates the tension between idealism and reality. Using art, Kiefer synthesizes this duality. In *Brunhilde Sleeps* he confronts ugliness in order to create beauty. He chooses the format of a book for this transformation. For more than two decades, books have been the artist's primary means for exploring subjects, techniques, and materials. By sequencing photographs in this intimate format and manipulating the images with various materials, he arrives at an almost alchemical distillation of reality, memory, and emotion. Here, Kiefer is able to stop time. He depicts the heroine in a somnolent, magical state, before passions are inflamed, before vows are made and broken, and preserves the moment when a happy ending still seems possible.

Carrie Przybilla

1. Quoted in Axel Hecht, "Macht der Mythen," *Art* 3 (1984), pp. 32–33.
2. This heroic epic poem was composed around 1200, probably by a minstrel poet in southern Germany, drawing on lost poems that may date back to the fifth century.

JIN SOO KIM

Korean, born 1950

Untitled; Integument, 1988–1991
Chenille bedspread, acrylic, Roplex, paper, and chair
50 × 19 × 22 inches
Collection of Janice Gold Dietz

Growing up in Korea in the aftermath of the Korean War, Jin Soo Kim was taught never to waste anything. Even the smallest scrap of paper was saved and eventually reused. Upon arriving in the United States at the age of twenty-four, she was fascinated and horrified by American consumer culture and the enormous amount of trash it generates. As Kim began to create sculpture here, she salvaged materials she found in gutters and dumpsters, incorporating them into her work. For her, recycling is not simply an artistic strategy but a psychological necessity, an attempt, she says to "reflect this society and the clash of my two cultures."[1]

Kim knew from an early age that she wanted to be an artist but initially chose the more practical course of becoming a nurse in order to support herself and her family. After arriving in the United States, she went to school to pursue a degree in art while still working as a nurse. To some extent, her medical background and artistic practice are inextricably bound. For example, the artist describes the armature of a sculpture as similar to the bones of the body. Kim's frequent use of plaster bandages in her work recalls the dressing of wounds, the care of broken limbs, and the preparation of corpses for burial. She intui-

tively incorporates the cycle of death, birth, and healing into her art, patiently urging her cast-off, spent materials toward redemption and new life.

Although best known for building enormous installations that form womb-like environments and meditative spaces, Kim has also created smaller, discreet objects that were never part of an installation, such as *Untitled; Integument.* She became interested in the ability of a chair to function as a surrogate body in 1984, and over the course of the next five years she created a series of works based on this fundamental form. Describing her process in making *Untitled; Integument,* she says, "I found this discarded kitchen chair in 1986 and after spending some time with the chair in the studio, I stripped it to its steel structure, its skeleton. I wrapped the armature of the chair as tightly as I could. The new integument combines the aspects of all the tissue layers, muscle as well as skin, yet remains incompletely revealed, bandaged and preserved."[2]

"Integument" is the medical term for skin. As the body's largest organ, it provides a surface that senses and interprets the external environment while protecting the interior of the body by maintaining body temperature, serving as a barrier to microorganisms, and conserving fluids. Kim's interest in this organ grew out of her recognition of the human body as a complex combination of systems and energy, most of which are invisible because of skin. The artist chose chenille to wrap the chair because in the form of a bedspread it already serves as a covering for the body and "seems to harbor a sense of warmth and protectiveness."[3] Her sculpture captures the energy of the body and the implied wonders within, yet like skin the chenille covering only hints at the internal structure as it clings to joints or bulges over hardware, in spots almost translucent but even then only slightly so. Kim leaves the back of the chair open to signal an incomplete narrative and resist any suggestion that the chair serves as some sort of portrait. Instead, she focuses attention on the contained strength of her figure, hoping viewers will viscerally identify with its energy.

Carrie Przybilla

1. Quoted in Eleanor Heartney, "United States: Jin Soo Kim," *ARTnews* 92, no. 5 (May 1993), p. 110.
2. Kim to Lenore Gold, 28 January 1994, copy, High Museum of Art, curatorial files.
3. Ibid.

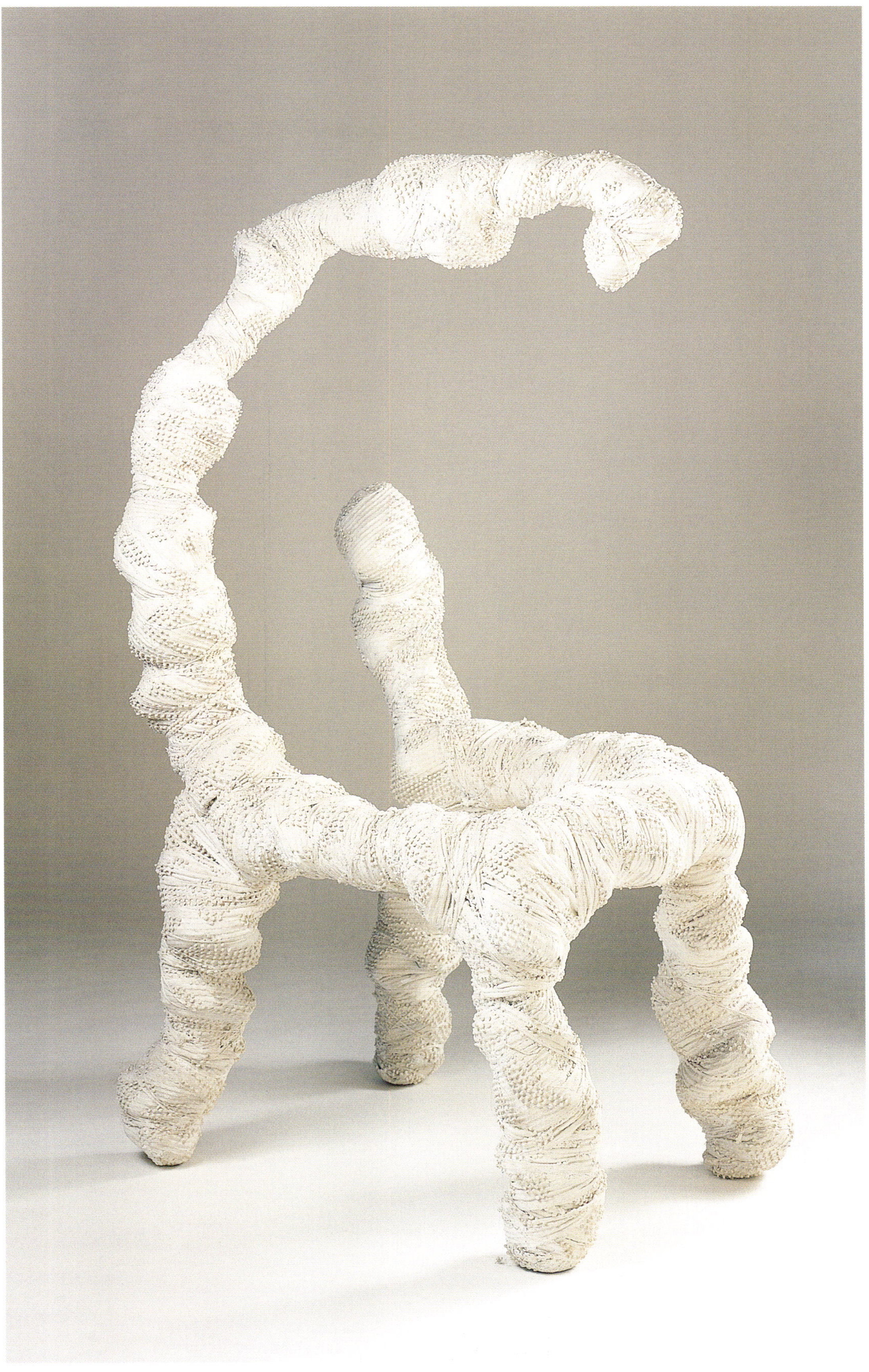

20

KOMAR & MELAMID

Vitaly Komar, Russian, born 1943
Alex Melamid, Russian, born 1945

10 Years Ago, 1978
Oil on canvas, paintbrush, dried plant, and Plexiglas
24¼ × 84½ × 4¼ inches
Collection of Burton Gold

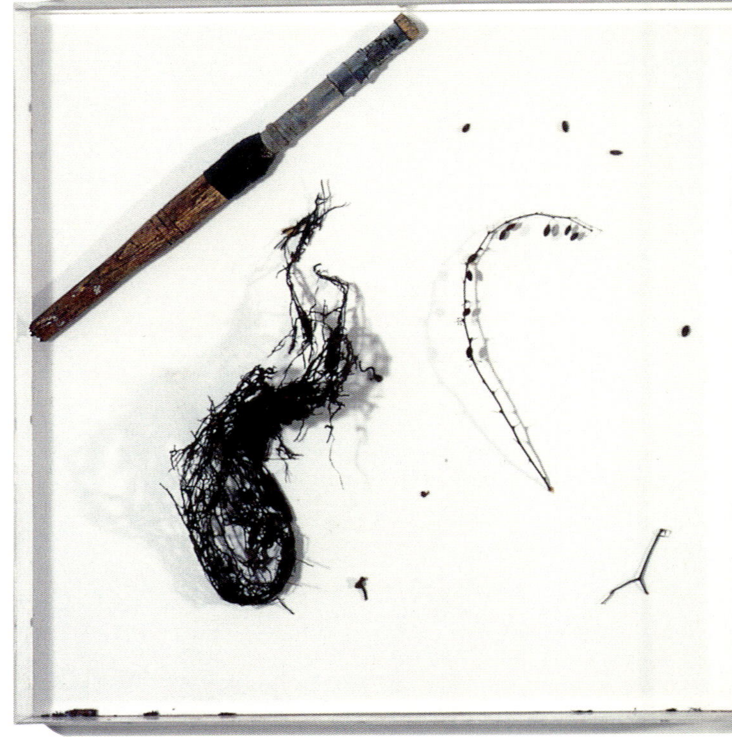

The Russian team of Komar and Melamid has been a mainstay in the contemporary art arena in the United States for well over two decades, and time has not blunted their caustic message. Always commenting on society, they use realist techniques to produce parody and are well known for their criticism of official Soviet politics, art, and culture. Since coming to the States in 1978, the themes they explore have broadened as the artists have become amalgamated into American culture. Regardless of the target, Komar and Melamid's work is consistent in its refusal to hold anything sacrosanct and its capacity to spur a reaction with its satire.

Vitaly Komar and Alex Melamid first met in a morgue during an anatomical drawing class at the Institute for Physical Culture in 1963 in Moscow. In 1965 they produced their first collabora-tion and have been partners ever since. In 1967, Komar and Melamid joined the youth section of the Moscow Union of Artists, from which they were later expelled "for distortion of Soviet reality and nonconformity with the principles of Socialist Realism."[1] Artists who did not conform to the standards of Socialist Realism were not allowed to work, nor were they given access to proper supplies or studio space.

Even before leaving the Soviet Union in 1977, Komar and Melamid had a following in the United States. They first attracted worldwide attention after participating in the infamous *Beljaevo* show, a one-day exhibition of art by twenty-four non-sanctioned Russian artists on 15 September 1974 in a vacant lot just outside of Moscow. Within min-utes Soviet authorities arrived on the scene, bull-dozing the area and destroying or seizing the art.

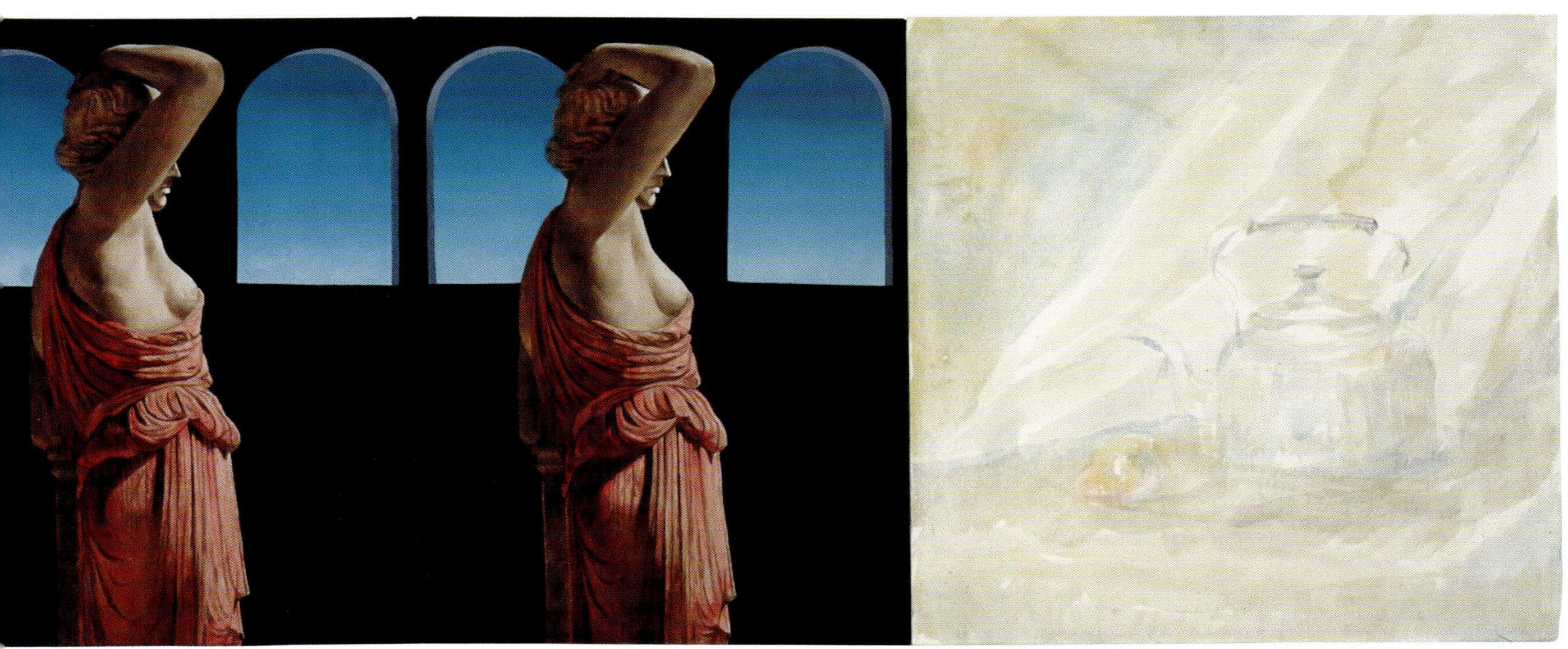

This episode generated much public outcry and support for the artists involved. In 1976, Komar and Melamid had their first exhibition in the United States. By 1977, the two artists renounced their Soviet citizenship, creating a "TransState," with its own constitution, alphabet, language, and currency. Soon after, the artists immigrated to Israel before settling in the United States in 1978.

Although Komar and Melamid embrace realism, their work stretches beyond the two-dimensional surface. It is conceptual and symbolic, simultaneously subtle and blatant. The artists' aim is to be provocative—to incite and ignite emotions, ideas, and laughter. They refer to historical figures and borrow iconography freely from classical subjects, monuments, and paintings, while they lambast long-established conventions and presuppositions of Western civilization.

10 Years Ago is a four-panel work. Inside Plexiglas, the left panel features a paintbrush, some intertwined weeds, and some indeterminate seeds floating on a white ground. On the right panel, there is a still-life drawing depicting a teapot. It is the two central panels that attract the most attention and trigger questions. Two identical figures stand in profile in front of a row of arches. Garbed in classical drapery, each form has her right arm poised overhead. Through the arches is a clear sky of deep blue. Not only is the shade of blue reminiscent of Surrealists Giorgio de Chirico and René Magritte, but there is a Surrealist quality to the entire composition. The unsettling silence and emptiness projected by the flat colors and pristine architectural elements work together with the figures to convey a sense of mystery and irony. Are these two women look-

ing back into the past or ahead to the future? Are the teapot and seeds symbols that indicate the traditional role of wife and mother that women held in society until feminism took root in the late 1960s? Certainly the title could reinforce that idea.

Trinkett Clark

1. Andrea Miller-Keller, "Vitali Komar and Aleksandr Melamid," in "MATRIX 43," exhibition brochure (Hartford, Conn.: Wadsworth Atheneum, 1978), unpaginated.

21

SOL LEWITT

American, born 1929

Twelve Forms Derived from a Cube, 1984

48 lithographs: 24 in black and 24 in
 four colors (edition 26/40)
Each image: 4 × 4 inches; each sheet: 8 × 8 inches
High Museum of Art, The Lenore and Burton Gold
 Collection of 20th-Century Art, 1987.120.1–48

Since the mid-1960s, Sol LeWitt has been in the vanguard of contemporary art. Associated with both Minimalism and Conceptual Art, he is well known for his abstract "wall drawings," sculpture, drawings, and prints, but it is his emphasis on the concept or idea of art rather than its physical realization that is perhaps his greatest legacy. In 1967, LeWitt wrote about his system of logic in *Artforum,* describing his

> search for a more objective method of organization as a reaction against the idea that art was composed with great sensitivity by the artist throughout the production of the work. This reaction eventually led to a theory of art that offered the idea that the original conception (perhaps intuition) of the work was of primary importance. . . . It proposed the notion of the artist as thinker and originator of ideas rather than as craftsman. Others, perhaps more able, could carry out the artist's design.[1]

LeWitt studied art at Syracuse University. After serving in Japan and Korea with the U.S. Army, he settled in New York in 1953, taking classes at the Cartoonists and Illustrators School (now The School of Visual Arts) and working as a commercial graphic designer.[2] Between 1960 and 1965, LeWitt worked in the bookstore and as a night receptionist at The Museum of Modern Art.[3] By the late 1960s, he was in the forefront of a burgeoning movement that rejected the emotion of the Abstract Expressionists in favor of an impersonal, detached, and minimal aesthetic based on geometric forms and pure colors.

LeWitt's reduced vocabulary incorporated elements such as the straight line, the square, and the cube. Discussing his affinity for the cube, he has said, "The most interesting characteristic of the cube is that it is relatively uninteresting. Compared to any other three dimensional form, the cube lacks any aggressive force, implies no motion, and is least emotive. Therefore it is the best form to use as a basic unit for any more elaborate function."[4] At the same time, LeWitt reduced his palette to black and white; later, he reintroduced primary colors in moderation. The artist was also intrigued with the sequential possibilities that a single form can generate. His work was directed by the idea that a shape could undergo endless permutations by adjusting just one simple element. Since the 1960s, LeWitt has focused on the infinite postures and progressions of the cube.

LeWitt began experimenting with drawings composed of lines moving in four directions— vertically, horizontally, and diagonally on opposite paths. This exercise resulted in the first of his many "wall drawings," presented in 1968 at the Paula Cooper Gallery in New York. Since his days as a student, he has dabbled with printmaking (etchings as well as lithographs and screen prints). In 1984, he produced a series of forty-eight lithographs depicting twenty-four different incarnations of the cube—one set of twenty-four in black and white, the other set in four colors that gradually change in range, hue, weight, and shape. Making an isometric projection of a cube, the artist exposes a cross-section, revealing an illusion of depth and perspective. Optical effects come into play with the gradient shades of black and white or shifting colors; this is further articulated by the four linear directions in the black-and-white prints, indicating perspective. When seen together, this group of forty-eight images comes to life as each cube transforms, merging harmoniously into the next iteration.

Trinkett Clark

1. Sol LeWitt, "Paragraphs on Conceptual Art," in *Sol LeWitt,* ed. Alicia Legg (New York: The Museum of Modern Art, 1978), pp. 166–167. First published in *Artforum* 5 (June 1967).
2. For a short time he worked on some projects for the architect I. M. Pei. This experience had an impact on LeWitt's philosophy about the confluence of art and architecture.
3. It is here that he met the art critic Lucy Lippard (who worked in the library) and fellow artists Dan Flavin, Robert Mangold, and Robert Ryman, who were museum guards.
4. Quoted in Lucy Lippard, ed., "Homage to the Square," *Art in America* 55, no. 4 (July/August 1967), p. 54, as cited in Michael Auping, "Sol LeWitt," in *Drawing Rooms: Jonathan Borofsky, Sol LeWitt, Richard Serra* (Fort Worth, Tex.: Modern Art Museum of Fort Worth, 1994), p. 15.

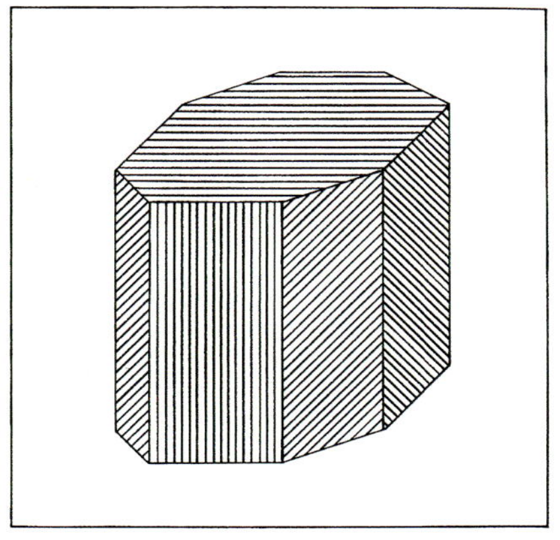

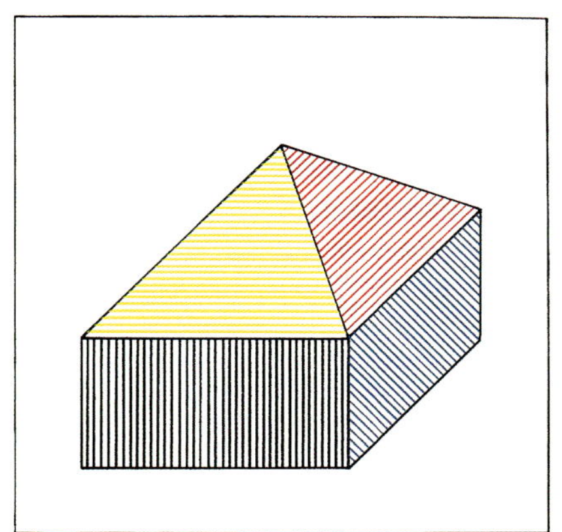

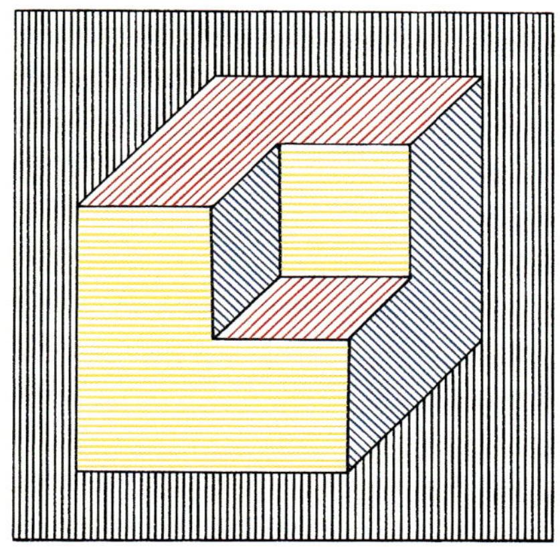

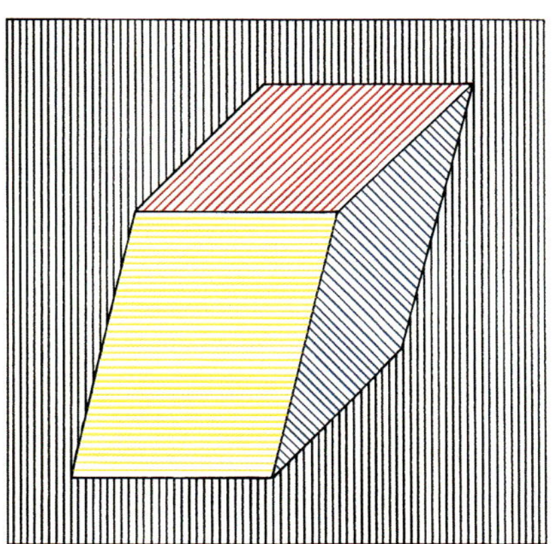

22

ROY LICHTENSTEIN

American, 1923–1997

Yellow Vase, 1991

Lithograph, woodcut, and screen print (edition 45/60)
49⅝ × 78½ inches
Promised gift of Burton Gold to the High Museum of
Art for The Lenore and Burton Gold Collection of
20th-Century Art

Roy Lichtenstein made his name as one of the central figures of Pop Art in the 1960s; his paintings based on romance and war comics and newspaper advertisements are among Pop's best-known images. Throughout his prolific career, Lichtenstein based his work on both high art and commercial sources, interpreting and transforming them, through his personalized, hard-edged style, into something entirely his own.

From 1991 to 1993, Lichtenstein created a series of paintings and prints of domestic interiors that were taken from advertisements in the yellow pages. The works depict undistinguished living or dining rooms with generic modern furnishings—in the case of *Yellow Vase,* a sectional couch, a standard square coffee table, a sleek floor lamp, a glass-topped table, and houseplants. The space is as anonymous and unlived in as a hotel room, an antiseptic, cartoon version of the American dream. Lichtenstein's interiors, like his Pop Art works, are supremely banal, both the rooms themselves and the origin of the images in the crudest type of ad.

Lichtenstein chose such forgettable subject matter because it allowed him to concentrate on the formal qualities of his work. He has said, "Once I have established what the subject is going to be, I am not interested in it anymore, although I want it to come through with the immediate impact of the comics."[1] The subject, while it is always recognizable, is simply a starting point, and Lichtenstein's works, with their tight compositions, spare style, and extreme simplification, border on the abstract.

A signature element of Lichtenstein's style is the pattern of dots that represents the halftone screen of benday dots used in commercial printing. The diagonal stripes recall the linear hatchings of engravings. These references to the mechanics of reproduction, which Lichtenstein incorporated into his work from his earliest Pop paintings, call attention to the prevalence of mass production in contemporary society. Even works of art, which we treasure largely because they are handcrafted, singular objects, are much better known to us through mechanical reproduction than through firsthand experience.

In his paintings and prints, Lichtenstein often alluded to his own work. Here, the shiny glass table in the foreground refers to his series of works depicting mirrors and reflections. Even the subject of domestic interiors was not new for him; his first interiors date from the early 1960s. The paintings Lichtenstein depicted hanging on the walls in the interiors are usually his own, but in this instance he quoted a famous image from another Pop artist, Andy Warhol's *Flowers,* 1964.

Anna Bloomfield

1. Quoted in Lawrence Alloway, *Lichtenstein* (New York: Abbeville Press, 1983), p. 73.

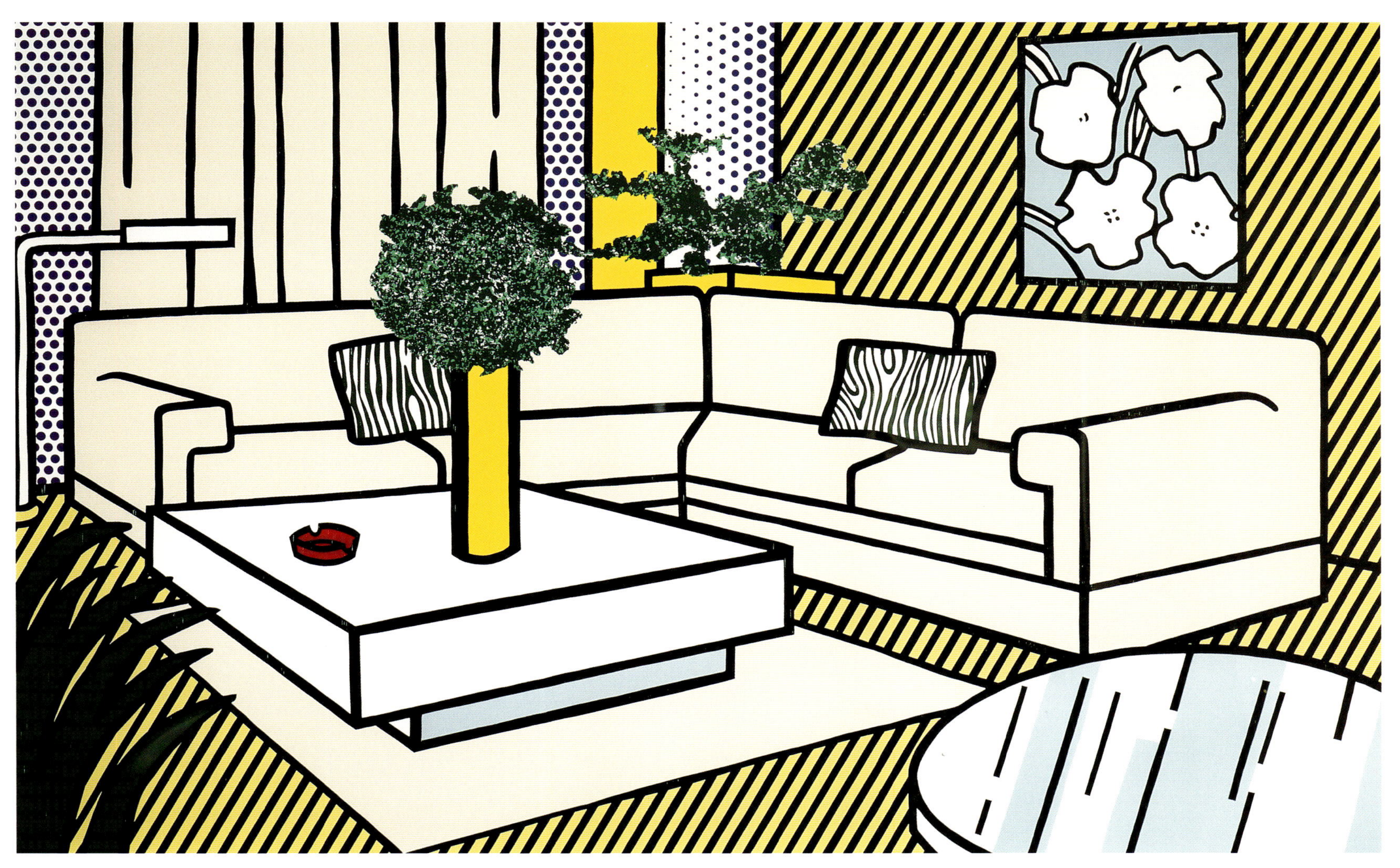

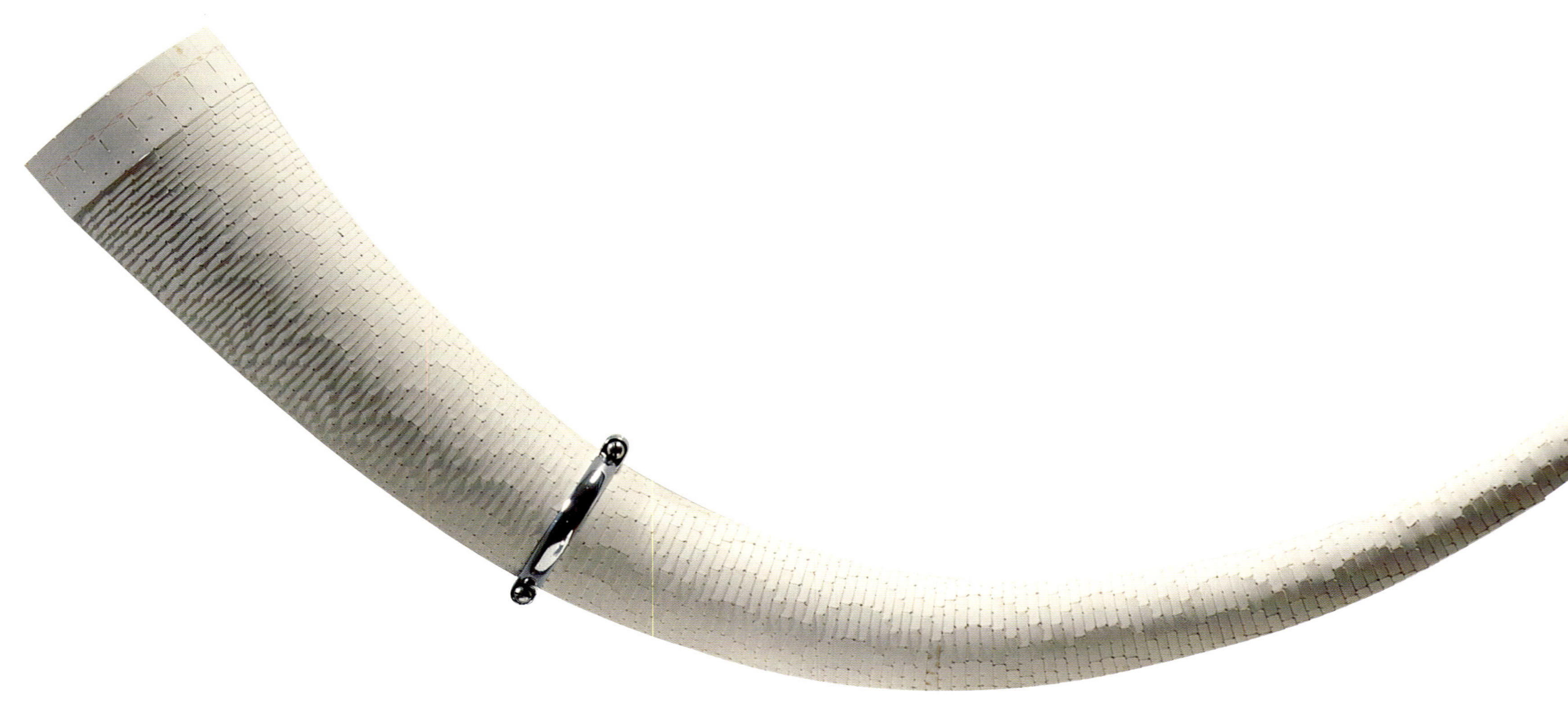

23

DONALD LIPSKI

American, born 1947

Price Tag #149, 1988
Paper, wood, aluminum, and steel
24 × 44 × 15 inches
Collection of Burton Gold

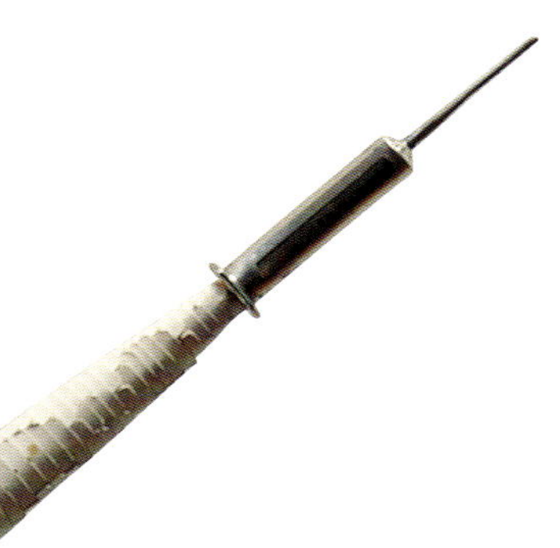

The true magician relies on the powers of suggestion, perception, and invention, drawing on an inner energy that transforms, captivates, and mystifies. An artist can be a magician, as Donald Lipski has demonstrated over the past twenty years. Both his individual assemblages and his installations have a magical effect. Freighted with irony and humor, his sculpture attracts, astounds, and mesmerizes.

Lipski grew up in Chicago, graduating from the University of Wisconsin at Madison in 1970. In 1973, he received an M.F.A. from the Cranbrook Academy of Art in Bloomfield Hills, Michigan. A quest for freedom activates and sustains Lipski's vision. Indeed, in 1979, after a visit to Bulgaria, where he saw artists limited by government-imposed rules, Lipski wrote, "I just started making stuff without thinking about any of the rules that we operate under, rules like 'just what is legiti-mate activity for an artist, what makes sense, what goes with what, what doesn't.'"[1]

Lipski's oeuvre falls outside of traditional parameters. He has ignored and subsequently redefined conventional concerns such as space, composition, and form; instead, he concentrates on the associative encounter, incorporating not just two or three dimensions into his work but the senses as well. Lipski seems able to look at a commonplace object—a bell, a flag, a plant, or a trumpet—and see beyond the obvious, revealing hidden potential. He recycles, revises, and revives the familiar, ready made object.

Lipski's sculptures of the late 1980s, including *Price Tag #149,* are sometimes poetic and contem-plative. Suspended in space, this long curvilinear work is made of white paper tags meticulously stacked and fanned to create a solid form that re-calls the bowed, curling shape of ancient horns or trumpets, in particular the shofar. This pure, aus-tere form first commands silence with its mystical, almost primal, presence. Upon closer scrutiny, the layers of price tags turn awe to laughter. The work transcends its utilitarian role as a horn and reflects the artist's wry, outrageous sense of in-vention in its use of the price tag as both medium and title.

Lipski fuses disparities, inviting the viewer to rethink traditional assumptions about art, society, and identity. Through his work, he transforms, captivates, and mystifies the viewer. Ultimately, Donald Lipski's sculpture goads us and forces us to explore the limits about what is sacred or irrev-erent, what is meaningful or irrelevant.

Trinkett Clark

1. Lipski, "Talking Objects: Interviews with Ten Younger Sculptors," interview by Wade Saunders, *Art in America* 73 (November 1985), p. 124.

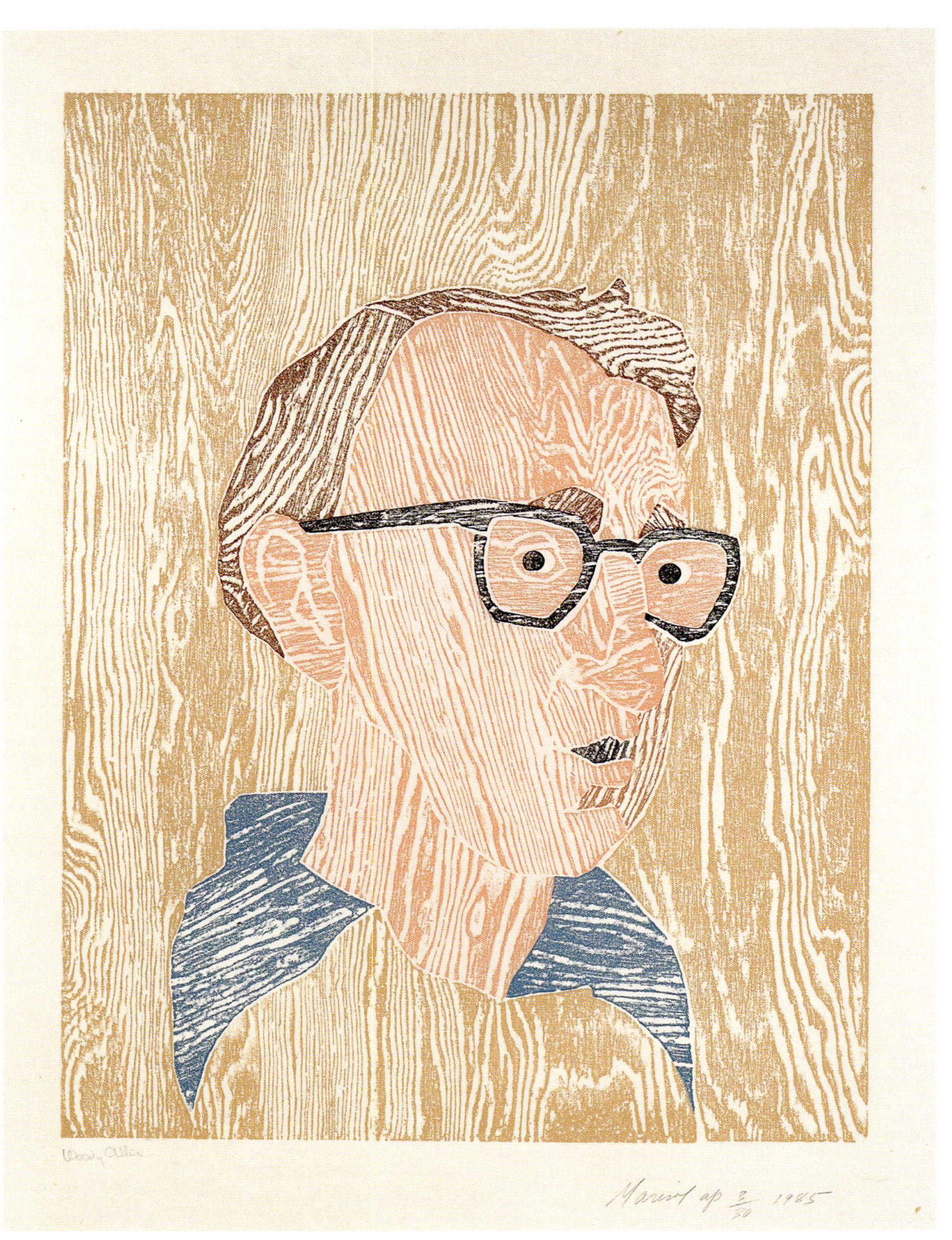

M A R I S O L

Venezuelan, born 1930

Woody Allen, 1985
Woodcut (artist's proof 3/30)
24 × 18 inches
High Museum of Art, The Lenore and Burton Gold
Collection of 20th-Century Art, given in honor of
the Board of Directors of the 20th Century Art
Society, 1984–1985, 1985.138

Marisol was the only female artist associ-
ated with the Pop Art movement of the 1960s,
but aside from the subtle, satirical humor and
topical content of her work during that period,
she had little in common with Pop artists. She
is best known for her portrait sculptures of celeb-
rities and heads of state, assemblages made from
discarded chunks of wood and other extraneous
elements that incorporate flat drawn and painted
surfaces.

Although Marisol calls her portraits "hom-
ages," they are not idealized or even particularly
flattering but, stopping just short of caricature,
seem to celebrate her subjects' idiosyncrasies.
Here film auteur Woody Allen, beady-eyed behind his familiar black-rimmed glasses, seems to
be talking, not posing. In fact, Allen did pose for
this portrait, uncharacteristically, which was commissioned by the City of Atlanta International Art
and Cultural Exchange at the time that his film
The Purple Rose of Cairo was released.

Marisol's prints are less known than her sculptures, yet she handles both media in similar ways.
This work is a woodcut, a type of relief print in
which flat wooden blocks (one for each color) are
carved, then inked and pressed onto paper. The
woodcut medium and her emphasis on the natural wood grain of the printing blocks refer to her
wooden sculpture and are also a pun on the

name of the sitter. Like her sculptures, the print
has the appearance of having been assembled
from various pieces of wood.

The print is signed by both the artist and the
sitter, two people notorious for claiming to be in-
tensely private, but who nonetheless consistently
feature themselves in their art. Marisol has frequently included self-portraits—plaster casts of
her face and hands, drawings, even bits of her
own clothing—in her sculptures, while Woody
Allen often appears in his own movies, always
seeming more or less to play himself. Marisol has
spoken of her art as a search for identity.[1] Making
portraits of other people might be seen as a way
of tempering her strong introspective impulse,
yet she often refers to herself indirectly in such
works (in this case, by alluding to her wood sculpture).[2] As she has said, "When I do a well-known
person . . . I am really doing myself."[3]

Anna Bloomfield

1. Paul Gardner, "Who Is Marisol," *ARTnews* 88, no. 5
   (May 1989), pp. 147–151.
2. Douglas Dreishpoon, "Marisol Portrait Sculpture,"
   Art Journal 50, no. 4 (Winter 1991), pp. 94–96.
3. Quoted in Leon Shulman, *Marisol* (Worcester, Mass.:
   Worcester Art Museum, 1971), unpaginated.

ALLAN McCOLLUM

American, born 1944

Perfect Vehicle #1629, 1989
MoorGlo on glass-fiber-reinforced concrete
78 × 36 × 36 inches
High Museum of Art, The Lenore and Burton Gold
  Collection of 20th-Century Art, 1999.111

Allan McCollum became an artist despite having little traditional artistic training, and he has never sought to develop the kinds of technical skills generally thought necessary to become a painter or sculptor. Rather, his interest lies in trying to understand what makes something art. A Marxist at heart, he is fascinated by the social position of the artist as laborer and the mystique of the unique art object. McCollum investigates how the meaning and value of a work of art vary according to the social, economic, and psychological context into which the work is placed.

When McCollum first conceived of the *Perfect Vehicle* in 1979, he sought to expose conventional assumptions about three-dimensional art objects. He began by collecting different types of jars to study their shapes and proportions, then experimented with different combinations of features. It took him six years to arrive at the final hybrid configuration, which most closely resembles a large ginger jar. But a *Perfect Vehicle* clearly has no function: the lid does not come off, and the six-and-a-half foot height is hardly a practical scale. Although produced in a limitless edition by McCollum's assistants and often shown in large groupings that emphasize their uniformity, each *Perfect Vehicle* is distinct. No two are colored exactly alike, and the artist conscientiously paints a small but unidentifiable portion of each. In so doing, he raises questions about the nature of originality and the value traditionally placed on the artist's hand. Similarly, McCollum uses commercial house paint to avoid creating the precious surfaces prized in ceramics, just as the weight and bulk of his concrete forms contradict the fragility typically ascribed to them. Thus, the opulence and exoticism long associated with fine ceramics, such as ginger jars, is replaced by a sense of quizzical irony. Because of McCollum's distortions of form and function, *Perfect Vehicle* acts as a caricature. It constitutes a sign for an artwork, which McCollum sees as key, noting that "an art object is in a way already a substitute for something else, so to make a substitute for a substitute is to foil its original function. This leaves a frightening but exciting sort of void."[1] Acting in the void they help to create, "the *Perfect Vehicles* are the most perfect art objects possible," says the artist. "They are irredeemably useless as vases since they are solid, and eminently 'useful' as the (substitute) Fine Art objects since they are used exactly for what they were intended."[2] That is, they raise questions about our definitions of art and creativity.

Carrie Przybilla

1. McCollum, "Interview with McCollum and Koons," interview by Daniela Salvioni, *Flash Art,* no. 131 (December 1986/January 1987), p. 68.
2. Ibid., p. 68.

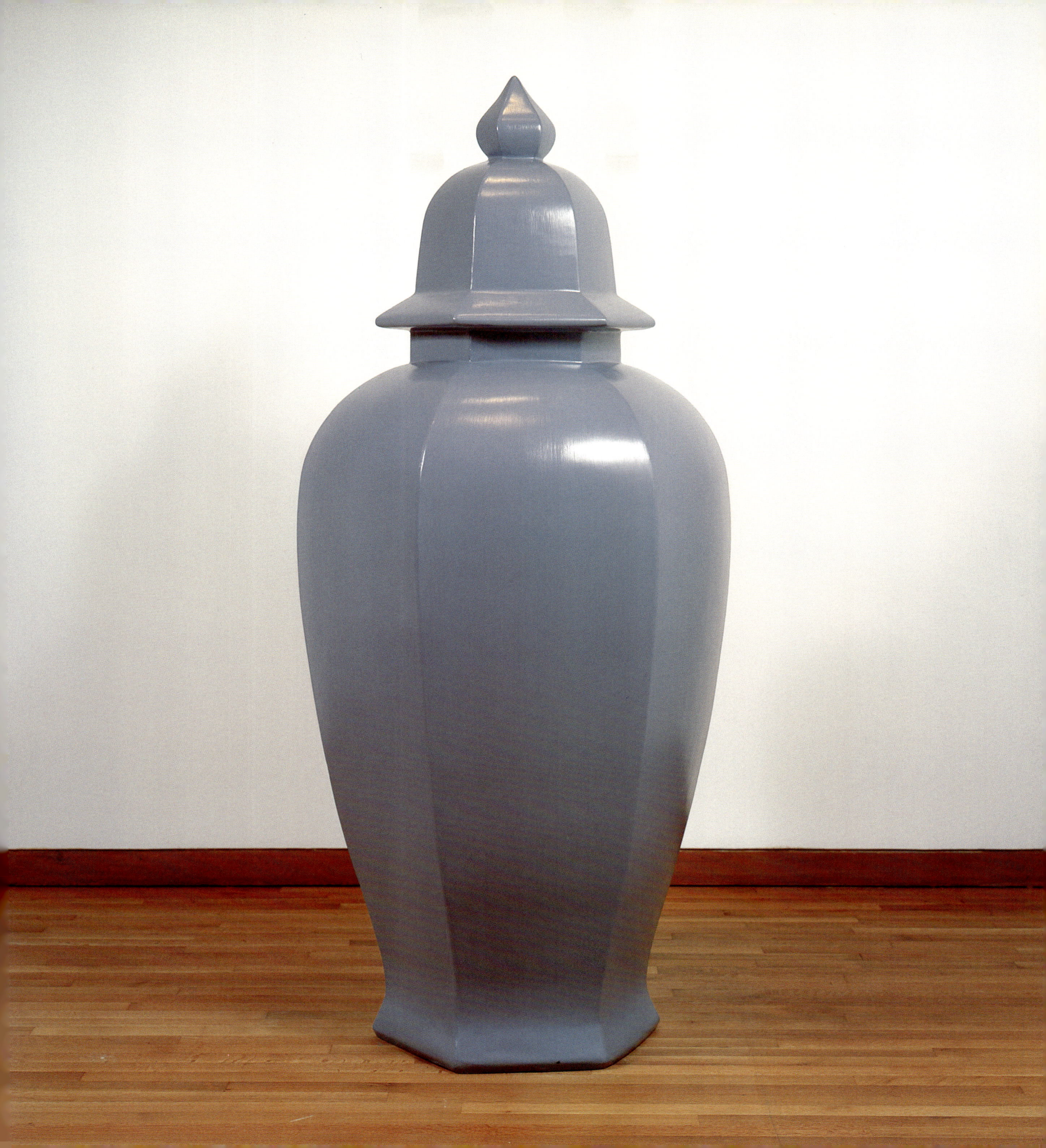

26

JOAN MIRÓ

Spanish, 1893–1983

Three Figures, 1935
Ink on paper
11½ × 8 inches
Collection of Burton Gold

The Catalan heritage of Joan Miró, who was born in Barcelona, was an enduring influence on his work throughout his long career. In the provincial and primitive artwork he saw growing up—prehistoric cave paintings, Catalan Romanesque murals, and Catalan Gothic retables —he observed simple, flat forms, a distortion of scale, and a fantastic, mythical quality, all of which would be apparent in his mature work.

Miró's earliest work was hard-edged, realistic, and highly detailed. When he moved to Paris in the early 1920s, he came to know a number of avant-garde artists, including some of the Surrealist painters and poets. Around this time he made a fundamental stylistic change and began working in the fanciful and radically reductive manner for which he is known. Miró is usually identified as a Surrealist; André Breton, author of *The Surrealist Manifesto,* famously called him "the most Surrealist of us all."[1] Miró, however, didn't really seem to align himself with this movement. Late in his life he countered, "A Spaniard does not need to be a Surrealist: he is already irrational."[2] He did, however, share some of the aims of the Surrealists, particularly that of freeing his work from the constraints of reason. Using accident

and irrational association, he allowed images to emerge without conscious control in order to express a purely intuitive and subconscious vision— a process the Surrealists called "pure psychic automatism."

In Miró's highly simplified style, people and objects are reduced to elemental, biomorphic signs. His work is never truly abstract, however, for each symbol refers to something concrete. In fact, he reacted with indignation when asked to join an abstraction group, "as if the signs that I transcribe on a canvas . . . were not profoundly real and did not belong essentially to the world of reality!"[3] The drawing *Three Figures,* for example, depicts three animated forms, perhaps dancing. The central figure is the largest and most detailed (it has breasts, a mouth, flowing hair), while the one to the right is more abbreviated, and the one to the left is scarcely recognizable as a human form. Typical of Miró, the figures have oversized feet, seeming to illustrate his 1947 statement, "We Catalans believe that your feet must be firmly planted in the ground if you want to leap into the air. The fact that I come down to earth again from time to time helps me to jump all the higher afterwards."[4] This statement

perfectly expresses the duality in Miró's work between grounded rationality and unbridled fantasy. Above the left figure is a star, an element Miró frequently included to signify the spiritual and celestial.

The inscription at the bottom of this drawing reads: "pour la Société Manès, en hommage de leur bel effort et en souvenir de cette agréable soirée, Miró—Prague 28/11/35."[5] Miró spent the last half of November 1935 in Prague for the opening of a group exhibition in which he was included. He apparently executed this drawing in appreciation to the organizers.

Anna Bloomfield

1. Quoted in Barbara Rose, *Miró in America* (Houston: The Museum of Fine Arts, Houston, 1982), p. 11.
2. Quoted in ibid., p. 11.
3. Quoted in ibid., p. 7.
4. Quoted in Henry T. Hopkins, *Joan Miró: Important Paintings, Sculpture and Graphic Works* (San Francisco: Harcourts Gallery, 1981), unpaginated.
5. For the Manès Society in appreciation for your fine effort and in remembrance of this pleasant party (author's translation).

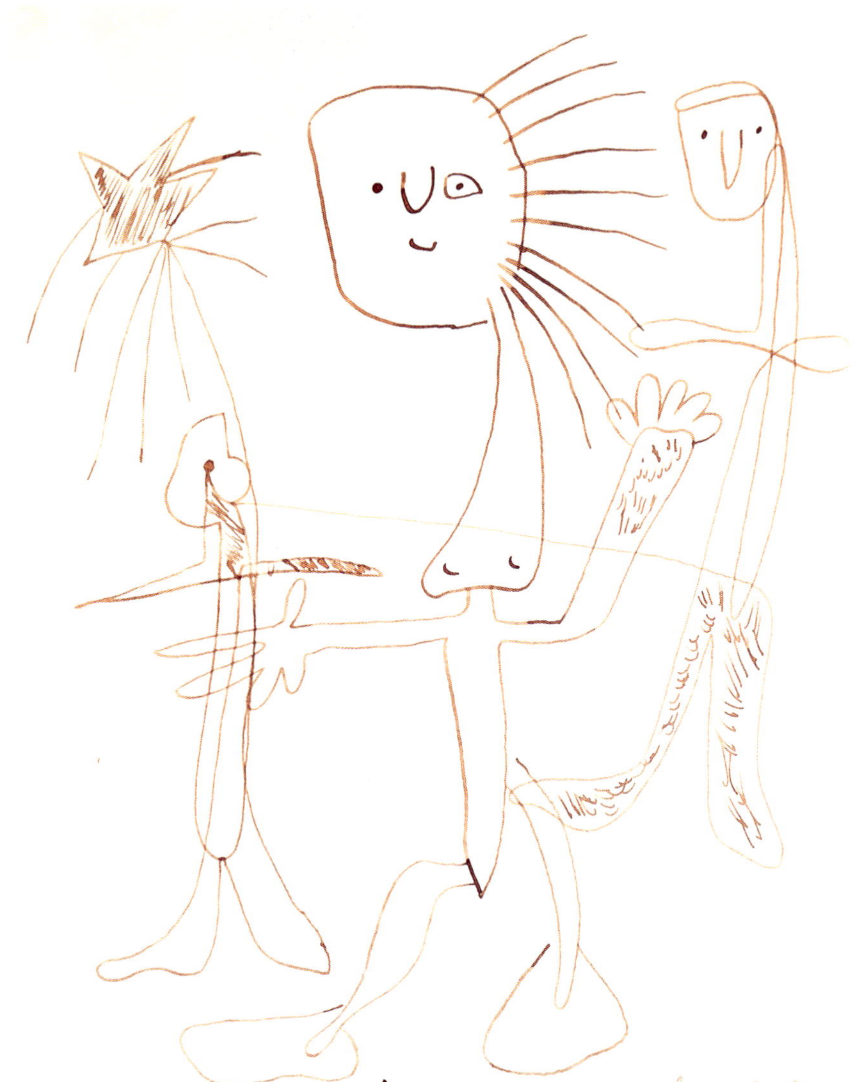

pour la Société manès, en hommage de leur bel
effort et en souvenir de cette agréable soirée,
Miró - Prague 28 / III / 35.

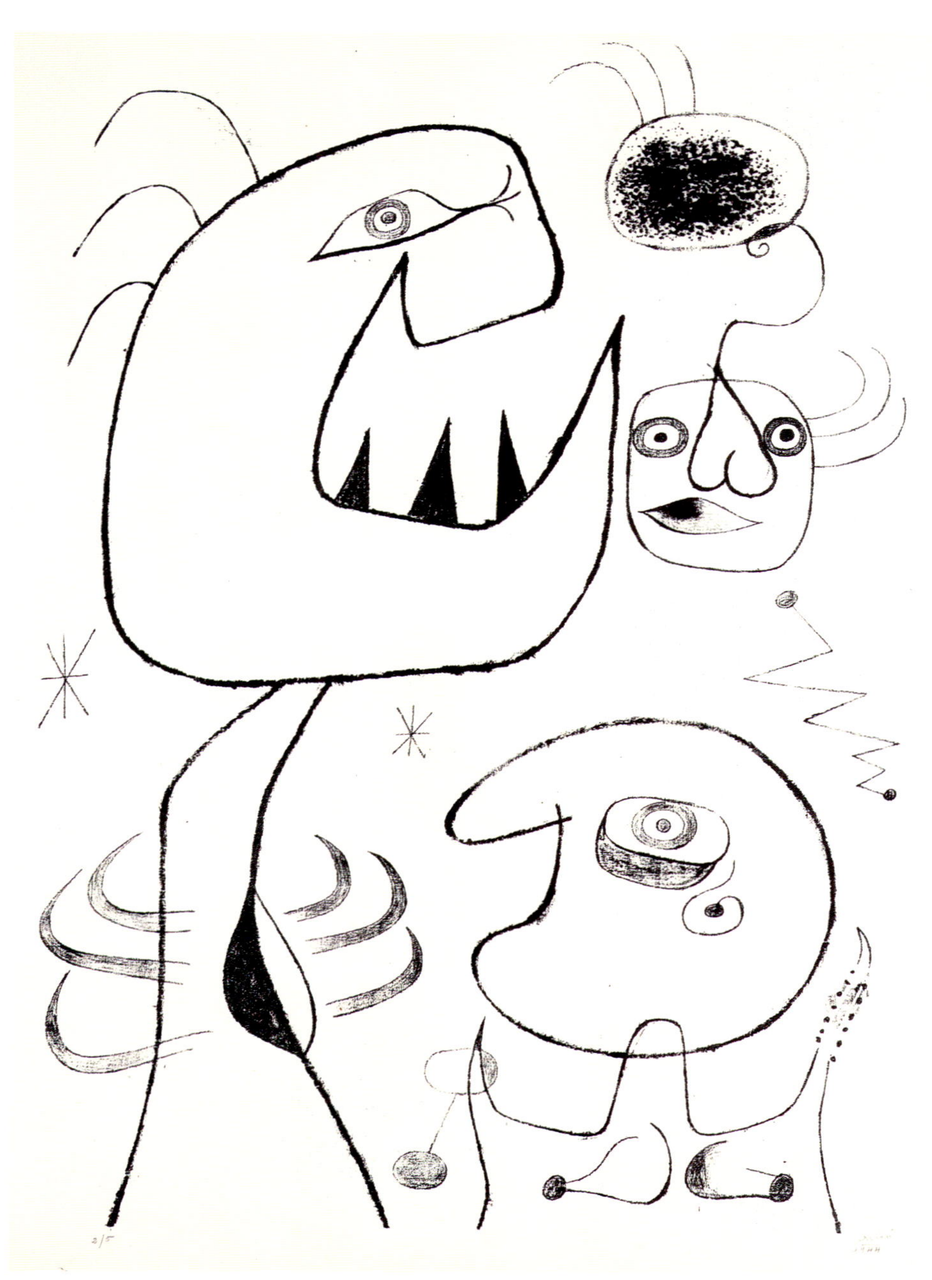

JOAN MIRÓ

Spanish, 1893–1983

Barcelona XVII, from the Barcelona Suite,
1944

Lithograph (edition 2/5)
26¼ × 19¼ inches
High Museum of Art, The Lenore and Burton Gold
    Collection of 20th-Century Art, given to mark the
    retirement of Gudmund Vigtel, 1991.277

During World War II, while many avant-
garde European artists took refuge in New York,
Joan Miró decided to return to Spain. The war
years were a period of difficulty and isolation for
the artist, when he wrote that "one must be
ready to work amidst total indifference and in
the most profound obscurity."[1] He returned to
the family farm and used his childhood nursery
for a studio, although he produced few paintings
due to the scarcity of materials. But as the war
drew to a close, Miró enthusiastically and vigor-
ously went back to work. One of the first projects
he completed was an important sequence of fifty
lithographs known as the Barcelona Suite, of
which this work is one.

Like *Three Figures* (cat. 26), this work also contains three characters, but much fiercer ones. The
large grimacing figure bares its sharp teeth and
roars; the symbol on its body may be raised arms
(six, like an insect) or may indicate a flaming
heart consumed by passion. The female figure
below and to the right casts a bleary-eyed gaze
outward and is connected by something resem-
bling a lightning bolt to a disembodied, flat-
nosed head, which is in turn connected by a hair
to an ominous, floating black form. Such violent
images may express Miró's frustration at his
forced hiatus during the war, or perhaps they are
the demons (rather charming, despite their feroc-
ity) that continually surface in his work.

Miró typically isolated and enlarged individual
elements in his work and set them afloat on flat,
empty fields with no indication of background
or horizon to ground them. For Miró, the infinite
space of the sky represented the spiritual realm
and was always of vital interest to him. As he
wrote in 1958, "The spectacle of the sky over-
whelms me. I'm overwhelmed when I see, in an
immense sky, the crescent of the moon, or the
sun. There are, in my pictures, tiny forms in huge
empty spaces. Empty spaces, empty horizons,
empty plains—everything which is bare has
always greatly impressed me. . . . I feel the need
of attaining the maximum of intensity with the
minimum of means. It is this which has led me to
give my painting a character of even greater
bareness."[2]

Anna Bloomfield

1. Quoted in Carolyn Lanchner, *Joan Miró* (New York: The
    Museum of Modern Art, 1993), p. 71.
2. Quoted in Dore Ashton, ed., *Twentieth-Century Artists
    on Art* (New York: Pantheon Books, 1985), pp. 9–10.

THE MOSSI PEOPLE

Burkina Faso

Mask and Costume

Wood, hemp, and medicine bag
82 × 24 × 22 inches
High Museum of Art, The Lenore and Burton Gold
   Collection of 20th-Century Art, 1992.224

This mask and costume are used by the Mossi people of the West African country of Burkina Faso (known during the French colonial era as Upper Volta). Around the fifteenth or sixteenth century, a group of Mossi rode north on horseback from what is now Ghana and established a new homeland in the basin of the White and Red Volta Rivers. In the process of resettlement, they conquered several ethnic groups and displaced others. The Mossi, then, are a heterogeneous people numbering over two million, whose diverse culture reflects the traditions, histories, and artistic styles of multiple groups.

Today, five hundred years after their migration, the Mossi still distinguish descendants of invading horsemen *(nakomse)* from descendants of conquered people *(tengabisi),* who include farmers, blacksmiths, weavers, and others. The *nakomse,* from whom kings and chiefs are chosen, traditionally use small-scale, sculpted portrait figures that represent the ruling family and/or their ancestors. The balance of power in Mossi society belongs to the *tengabisi,* who hold positions of religious and spiritual authority such as earth priest and lineage head. Masquerade, a performance art central to the functioning of society, was practiced by the indigenous people of the Volta basin at the time of the Mossi conquest, and it is still practiced and governed by the *tengabisi.*[1]

Masquerade, which combines dance, drumming, and ritual, serves as a means of connecting the community to the world of ancestors, as well as to totemic animal spirits associated with mythic origins of each clan. Performances occur at funerals, initiations, and at various important points of the agricultural cycle. Although both the male and female genders are represented in masks, all masks are worn by men. In certain Mossi regions, women are active audience members and dance alongside the masks, but in the Boulsa region women are not permitted to participate in the performances.[2]

This mask type, belonging to a category called *gur-wando,* comes from the eastern Mossi region around the village of Boulsa. The mask represents a male character called *wan-zego* (red mask) and is identified by the white pigment on the face and the red hemp costume.[3] There are two other characters in this masquerade group: a female, who wears a black hemp costume and whose mask is covered with red seeds, and a dwarf, whose mask has vertical horns. The dwarf mask is the most powerful of the three and is protected by the male mask in performance.[4] The *wan-zego* character usually holds a knife or a whip, and a bag of powerful traditional medicine is suspended by a rope from the tall hemp headdress atop the mask. Masked characters in performance do not speak in human voices but communicate with reed whistles that are held between the teeth.

Among the Mossi and other ethnic groups in Burkina Faso, masks generally embody divine forces and divine law and are deeply respected in rural village communities. Although the period of French colonial rule and subsequent establishment of independent African nations in West Africa engendered profound social, political, and

cultural changes, masquerade continues to serve
as one of the centerpoints of Mossi culture, re-
minding people of their origins and histories and
allowing for interaction between the visible and
invisible worlds. Masks such as this have also become an important part of Burkina Faso's national
cultural patrimony and are included in cultural
festivals that are attended by international
audiences.[5]

Emily G. Hanna

1. See Christopher Roy, *Art of the Upper Volta Rivers*
   (Meudon, France: Alain and Francoise Chaffin, 1987),
   pp. 90–191.
2. Ibid., p. 145.
3. Ibid., p. 140.
4. Ibid., p. 138.
5. Emily Hanna-Vergara, "Masks of Leaves and Wood
   among the Bwa of Burkina Faso," (Ph.D. diss., University of Iowa School of Art and Art History, 1996),
   pp. 170–173.

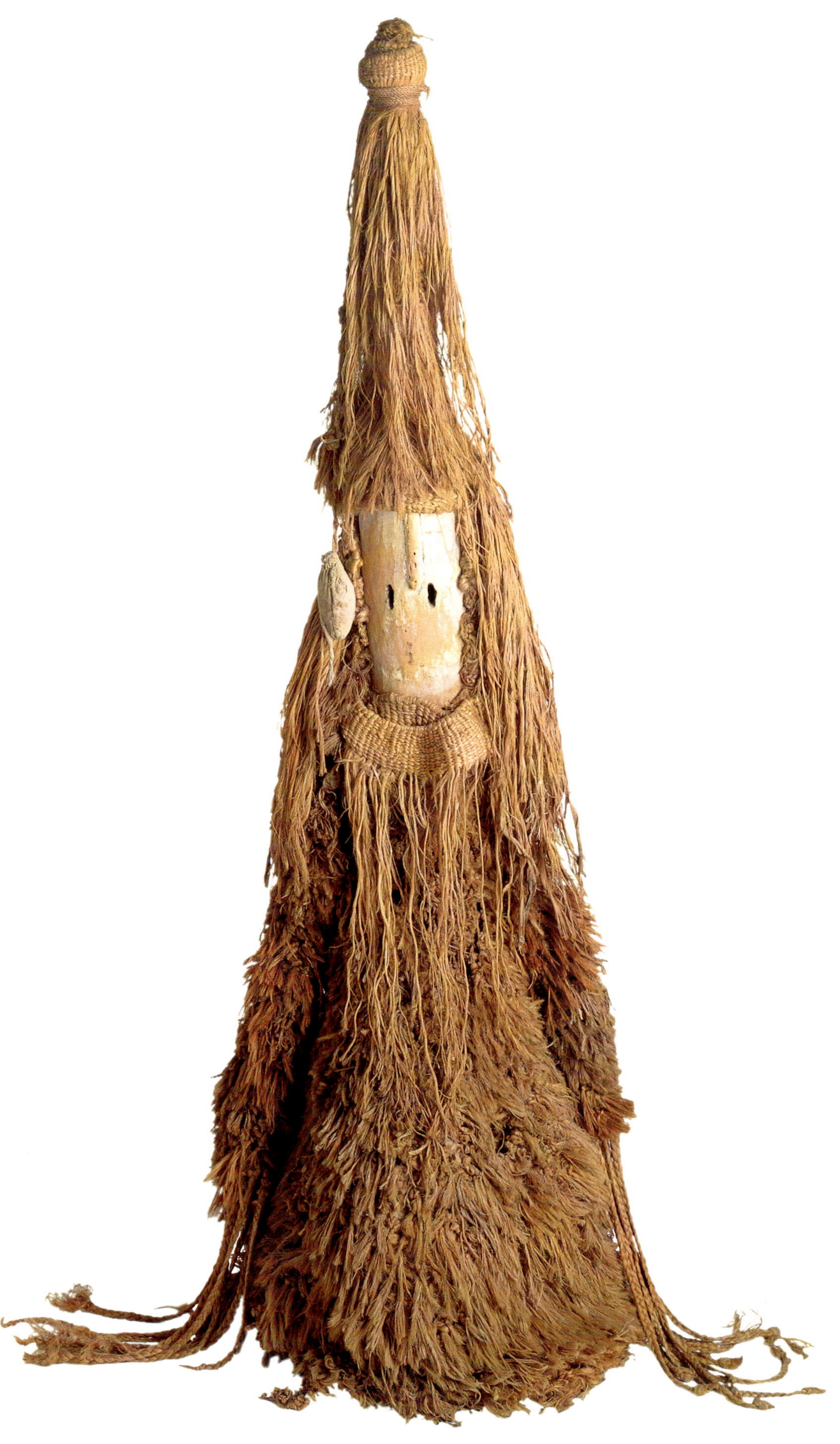

29

LOUISE NEVELSON

American, born Russia, ca. 1900–1988

Shadows, 1959

Paint on wood
77 × 27 × 4 inches
Collection of Lauren G. Grien

The shadow, you know, is as important as the object. . . . I arrest it and I give it architecture as solid as anything can be.

—Louise Nevelson[1]

Louise Nevelson led an unorthodox and col- orful life, particularly for a woman of her generation. When she was a child her family emigrated from Russia and settled in rural Maine. She married a wealthy man when she was twenty and moved to New York. Quickly bored with her life as a homemaker and mother, Nevelson took lessons in painting, acting, and singing. In 1929 she enrolled in courses at the Art Students' League. She abandoned her unhappy marriage in 1931 and went to Munich to study with Hans Hofmann because of his reputation as an innovative teacher. While there, Nevelson traveled to other European cities in order to see as much art as she could. In the course of her journeys, she appeared as an extra in several Austrian feature films. She returned to New York in 1932 and was introduced to Diego Rivera by a mutual friend. Rivera hired Nevelson to assist him with a series of murals he was then producing in the city. At the same time, she took up the study of dance, which she would pursue for the next two decades, and returned to classes at the Art Students' League, where Hofmann was then teaching. Nevelson began exhibiting her work in New York in the mid-1930s, but it wasn't

until the late 1950s, when she was nearly sixty, that her signature assemblage sculptures began to receive critical acclaim. Finally, during the last quarter of her long and productive life, she was able to support herself through the sale of her work, which was the subject of numerous exhibitions in the United States and abroad.

Nevelson created *Shadows* just as her work was beginning to receive recognition, and it exemplifies her mature style. She worked primarily in wood—although at times she also employed metal, paper, Plexiglas, and fabric—and composed her sculptures spontaneously, constructing boxes and compartments into which she placed a variety of found objects. She viewed her work as a collection of elements constantly at play, a never-ending dialogue of juxtaposed relationships, and used the interplay of light and shadow to establish a silent cadence of shape and interval. By gathering fragments into a complex assemblage and painting them a single color, the artist obscured the original identity of her disparate elements and unified them formally, transforming mundane bric-a-brac into enchanting and mysterious structures. Over the years, she developed a palette that included white and gold, but she always favored the black of works such as *Shadows,* declaring that "black is the most aristocratic color. I've always maintained that black contains all colors, because there

are no two blacks that are alike. You can go to Woolworth's and find some junky thing and if you paint it right in black it will take on greatness."[2]

Nevelson brought elements from Cubism, Constructivist painting, and color field painting into her work. She was the first postwar sculptor to produce work whose scale and allover compositions could be compared to those of Abstract Expressionist painting, and the result changed perceptions about scale in contemporary sculpture. Her works, both deep and frontal, occupy a zone halfway between the flatness of painting and the roundness of sculpture. Because the viewer cannot read their individual elements without musing on their origins, her pieces also seem to float between the real and the abstract, the poetic and the factual, the antique and the new, reflecting the multiplicity of contemporary life.

Carrie Przybilla

1. Quoted in Jean Lipman, *Nevelson's World* (New York: Hudson Hills Press in association with the Whitney Museum of American Art, 1983), p. 83.
2. Quoted in Carol Diehl, "Breaking the Rules," *Art & Antiques* (April 1988), p. 74.

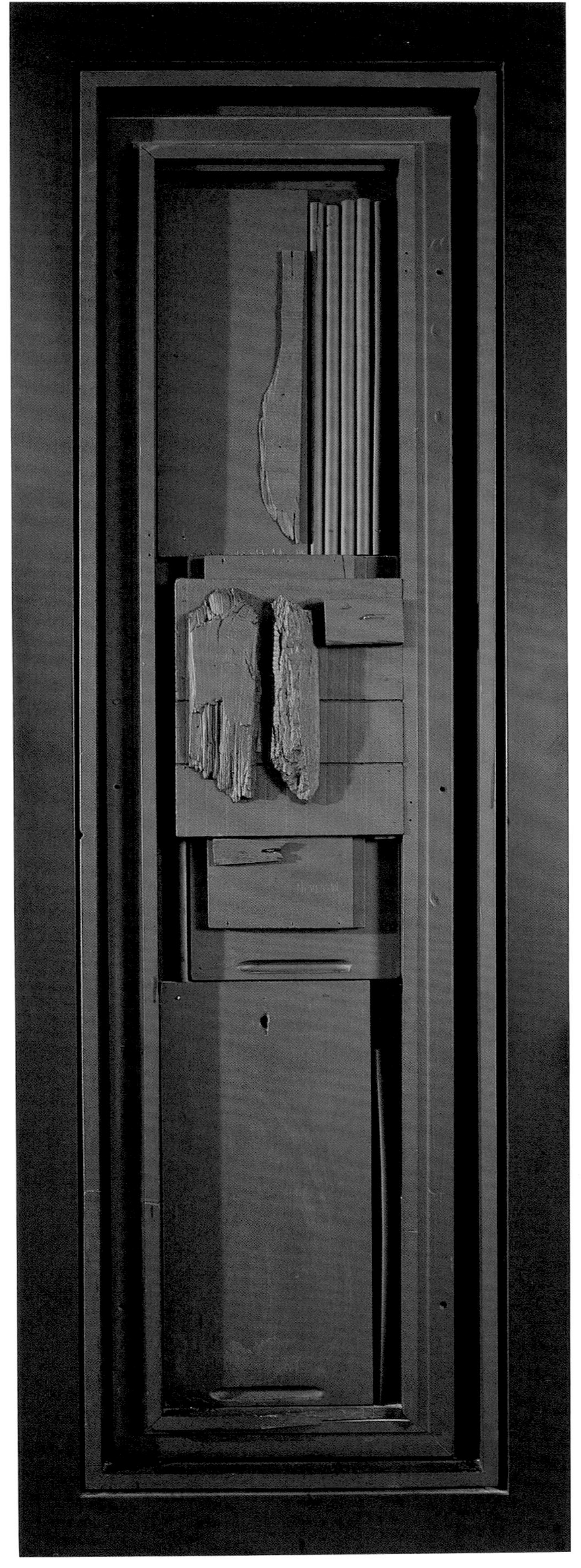

30

RICHARD NONAS

American, born 1936

Steel Drawing, 1990

Pigment on steel
Four panels, each 72 × 24 inches; installed dimensions variable: approximately 71 × 96 × 10 inches
Collection of Burton Gold

Richard Nonas did not set out to be an art-ist. In fact, he had been an anthropologist for about ten years when he decided to redirect his energies toward art in 1966. After two years of fieldwork in northern Mexico, where he was compiling data for a book about the Papago Indians, Nonas returned to his native New York uneasy and dissatisfied with his voyeuristic role. Upon his return to the city, he walked his dog in Central Park every day and found himself taking home pieces of wood strewn along his path. One day Nonas put two pieces together and the configuration triggered an aesthetic impulse that had profound resonance. He realized that art was a means of direct communication of emotion. By employing visual materials instead of words, abstract ideas could be conveyed succinctly and with an intense impact. Since this epiphany, Nonas has been an artist, using wood, stone, and steel as his vocabulary.

As a starting point, Nonas prefers common, ordinary materials: "Everyone is familiar with the properties of steel, for instance. It's cold, it's hard, it's heavy, it's easily obtained. In a sense, there is a lack of mystery to steel. I rely on this, and a clarity of construction. It is the way these materials are put together that achieves the emotional power I want. It is only when you step back that all the parts make a whole and the work becomes a vibrant presence."[1]

Nonas refers to his extensive travels as a way of describing his aesthetic intention. The need to re-create that sublime and unexpected sense of wonder and emotion for a particular place—a clearing in a forest, the wide expanse of a desert—is something that often propels an artist. It is this emotional "power of place, sense of presence" that Nonas is trying to capture in his work. He is concerned with the overall impact of his work and its potential ability to transform the space and the viewer: "I'm interested in the power of an object and its ability to shift a place. I'm not interested in making objects. I see my work as a tool that helps to change one's view of the world, maybe just for a moment, but in a profound way."

Steel Drawing is from a series that Nonas began in 1988. Four steel panels, all the same shape and size, lean side by side against a wall. In this work, Nonas explores the space where the floor meets the wall, explaining,

> We're used to the boundaries of an enclosed interior space. The floor encompasses the domain of gravity. The wall is free from gravity. But there are in-between spaces. This piece involves both the floor and the wall. A sculpture has weight, a painting floats on the wall. Therefore, I call this a drawing. This piece is about oppositions, weight versus levitation, red versus yellow. It's not on the floor or hanging on the wall. It leans against the floor and pushes against the wall. One of the most interesting elements is the compressed air behind the steel planes.

Steel Drawing suggests strength and authority, energy and balance, distance and intimacy, generating a frozen moment that leads to reflection and curiosity.

Trinkett Clark

1. Richard Nonas, conversation with the author, 16 May 2000. All quotations are taken from this conversation.

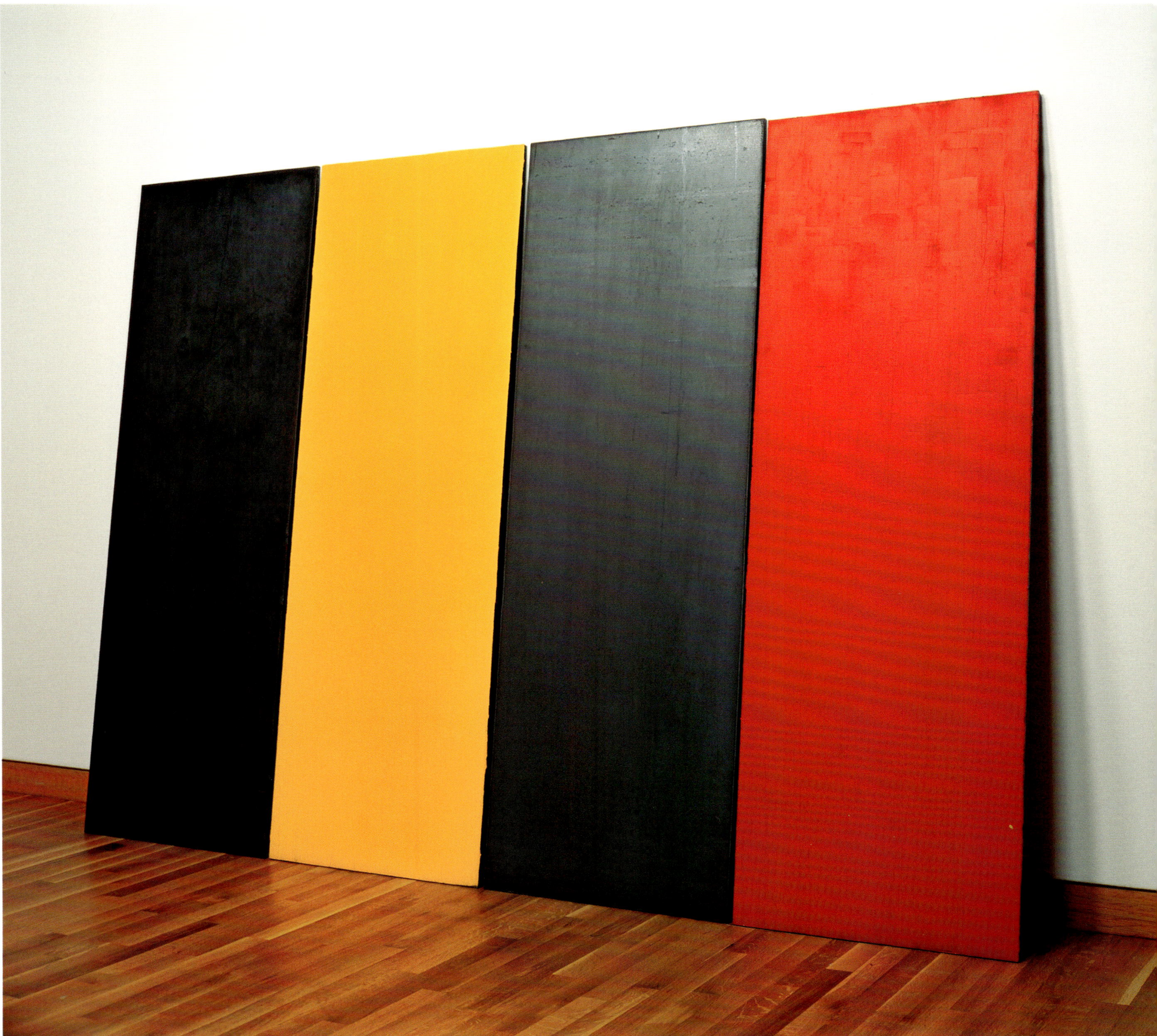

31

JULES OLITSKI

American, born Russia, 1922

Untitled, 1963

Acrylic on canvas
45 × 54 inches
Collection of Burton Gold

Jules Olitski's primary concerns lie with the process of painting, the relationships between colors (particularly those of similar hues), and the experience that the resulting composition provides for the viewer.

Olitski was born in 1922 in Snovsk, Russia (now Shchors, Ukraine), shortly after his father was executed as a political dissident. Born Jevel Demikovsky, Olitski immigrated to New York with his mother and grandmother in 1923. In 1926, his mother married Hyman Olitsky; years later, he changed his name to that of his stepfather, revising the spelling in 1958.[1]

From an early age, Olitski displayed an interest in art, making drawings inspired by newspaper photographs. In 1935, he began taking art classes on Saturday mornings, and from 1939 until 1942 he studied painting at the National Academy of Design and Sculpture at the Beaux-Arts Institute. After serving in the army in World War II, Olitski returned to the States until 1949, when he settled in Paris to pursue his artistic training. Under the auspices of the GI Bill, Olitski studied academic painting and drawing at the Académie de la Grande Chaumière and sculpture with Ossip Zadkine.

By 1951 Olitski was back in New York, where he began exploring abstraction, using heavily applied impastos and subdued colors. Although he had participated in a few exhibitions, it was a show in 1959 that led to a shift in his career. The critic Clement Greenberg, who was working as a consultant for French & Company, a new gallery in New York devoted to contemporary art, invited Olitski to have a solo exhibition. During the course of the show, the artist was introduced to the painter Kenneth Noland, as well as other members of the avant-garde.[2]

By the early 1960s, Olitski began to make his mark, exploring the nature of color and entering the vanguard of younger color field painters that included Helen Frankenthaler, Morris Louis, and Kenneth Noland. Using raw, unprimed canvas and acrylic resins, Olitski applied color by pouring paint directly onto the surface. The color soaked and stained the absorbent canvas, and abstract, amorphous shapes bled onto an open field. This painting, with its cropped, circular blue form, green inner circle, and echoing orange arc, is vibrant, yet contemplative, made so by the minimal number of components and colors and the white, empty space. This work is typical of Olitski's style during the early 1960s with its spare composition, organic forms, and vivid palette.

In 1963, Olitski joined the art department at Bennington College in Vermont; he was there at an extraordinary moment in the college's history. Together with Noland, Anthony Caro, Paul Feeley, David Smith (who lectured periodically at Bennington), and others, Olitski became one of the artists who contributed to the school's rich artistic legacy. At the same time, these artists shared ideas, providing encouragement and stimulating new work. Certainly the circular elements of this work recall Noland's target compositions. Soon after meeting Caro, both Noland and Olitski began to work in three dimensions, experimenting with steel and aluminum.

Within a year of arriving at Bennington, Olitski embarked on a new direction, asserting his independence. His paintings executed in 1964 were stained from top to bottom. Using a roller, Olitski stained his unprimed canvas with monochromatic "curtains" of color and emphasized the edges with contrasting hues. From this stage, the next evolution in Olitski's artistic career—and perhaps his signature style—developed naturally.

Trinkett Clark

1. Olitski served in the U.S. Army between 1942 and 1945. During that time he became an American citizen and changed his last name.
2. Andrew Hudson, "Caro, Noland, Olitski," *Fifteen Sculptors in Steel Around Bennington: 1963–1978* (North Bennington, Vt.: Park-McCullough House Association, 1978), unpaginated.

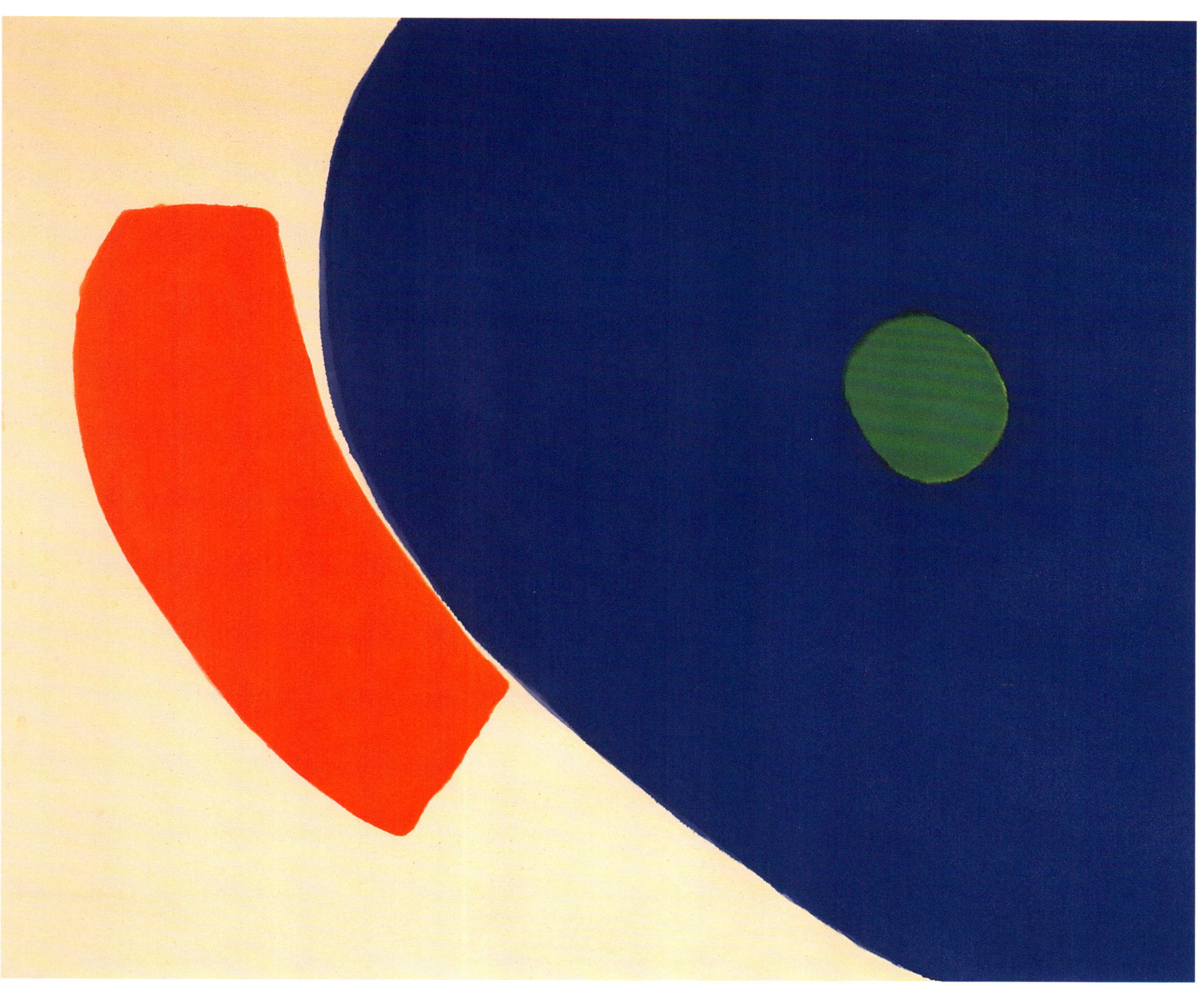

32

JULES OLITSKI

American, born Russia, 1922

Larro II, 1972
Acrylic on canvas
83¾ × 81 inches
Collection of Burton Gold

By 1965, Olitski's paintings had undergone a dramatic change. Another artist from the Bennington group had influenced him. Although known primarily as a sculptor, David Smith always considered himself to be first and foremost a painter.[1] In 1958, Smith began experimenting with spray paint, and his sprayed enamel paintings and drawings are remarkable for their iridescent texture and atmospheric spatiality. Olitski was aware of these works but was not inspired by them. It was not until the mid-1960s that Olitski, with a different goal in mind, became intrigued by the technique of spray paint. Matthew Collings reports Olitski remembering a conversation he had had in the Bennington days with Caro and Noland:

> Caro said he was interested in weight and materiality, in density, and Olitski suddenly realized he was interested in the opposite. He would like it if he could do a painting where colour just seemed to hang in the air like a light spray. The thought kept him awake that night and the next day he went to the shop . . . and bought the machinery. . . . The heavy industrial spray machines shot him around the studio a bit at first but then he got the hang of them and was even able to use two at a time, "Like the Westerns—two guns!"[2]

Working directly on the floor, Olitski sprayed clouds of paint into the air, the billowing plumes of color settling onto unprimed, unsized canvas. The result, large fields of mottled colors, conveys an ethereal sense of depth, space, and chiaroscuro. Shortly after Olitski began working with spray guns, he was selected by Henry Geldzahler to represent the United States at the 1966 Venice Biennale along with Helen Frankenthaler, Ellsworth Kelly, and Roy Lichtenstein. In a statement he prepared, Olitski said, "I think of painting as possessed by a structure—i.e., shape and size, support and edge—but a structure born of the flow of color feeling. Color *in* color is felt at any and every place of the pictorial organization; in its immediacy—its particularity. Color is felt throughout."[3]

In 1968, Olitski began to experiment even more with his surfaces, adding gel to his acrylic medium to give it volume and combining the paint with varnish and metallic and pearlescent powders in order to achieve greater texture.[4] By 1972 his attention had turned to the hidden surface beneath the layers of spray. Using mops, rollers, squeegees, and brooms, the artist manipulated his pigment before deploying the final skin of spray paint. *Larro II* is a classic example of Olitski's experiment. Depending on the light and the position of the viewer, the stippled atmospheric surfaces shimmer and radiate—in a sense, reproducing the process of flecks of paint floating in space. The grays can shift to lavender or pink, flooding the viewer in an aura of color while playing optical games. It is difficult to actually separate the specks of color in one's mind. The colors oscillate, simultaneously moving forward and backward. Like most of Olitski's work from this period, *Larro II* makes both a visual and cerebral impact upon the viewer.

Trinkett Clark

1. Smith, "Self-Portrait of an American Sculptor," interview by David Sylvester, British Broadcasting Corporation, 16 June 1961. A tape and transcript are housed at the Archives of American Art, Smithsonian Institution, Washington, D.C. See also Trinkett Clark, *The Drawings of David Smith* (Washington, D.C.: International Exhibitions Foundation, 1985), p. 18.

2. Collings, "'What's it like to be forgotten?' Jules Olitski interviewed," *The Art Newspaper* X, no. 97 (November 1999), p. 40.

3. Olitski, "Painting in Color," in Henry Geldzahler, *Helen Frankenthaler, Ellsworth Kelly, Roy Lichtenstein, Jules Olitski, XXXIII International Biennial Exhibition of Art Venice* (Washington, D.C.: National Collection of Fine Arts, Smithsonian Institution, 1966), p. 39.

4. See John Elderfield, *Frankenthaler* (New York: Abrams, 1989), p. 296.

33

MIMMO PALADINO

Italian, born 1948

Room in a Tempest, 1984

Oil on canvas, wood, and found objects
95½ × 104 × 5 inches
High Museum of Art, The Lenore and Burton Gold
  Collection of 20th-Century Art, 1999.106

Mimmo Paladino's work forms a bridge between the conceptual thrust of the Italian *arte povera* movement in the late 1960s and early 1970s and the *trans-avantegardia,* which critic Achille Bonito Oliva defined as a return to classical techniques and media with an emphasis on imagery. Along with compatriots Sandro Chia, Enzo Cucchi, and Francesco Clemente, Paladino played a key role in this international revival of emotionally charged, figurative painting, drawing, and sculpture in the late 1970s and early 1980s. Filled with symbolism and enigmatic narrative, his work explores psychological states and their relationship to the whole of human cultural expression. The artist draws from a complex, multilayered reservoir of subjects and styles that encompasses a wealth of past civilizations. Assimilated and transformed, his formal and thematic references remain intentionally elusive and cannot be attributed to any single time or place. Paladino shuns specific interpretations of his work, preferring to let viewers decipher meaning for themselves. "The figures in my paintings," he says, "the animals, the masks, the theme of death—I do not want to explain or analyze them. They are the roots out of which the picture develops, but not its content. That is an entirely different area which also cannot be researched with the methods of art criticism . . . because the artist always plays his game of hiding what might be evident."[1]

The ambiguous narrative and rich symbolism in *Room in a Tempest* present a variety of possible readings. Although the thickly painted canvas reveals few details of the setting, several stylized faces emerge from the background and seem to hover around the crouching figure at the center of this enormous composition. Are they ghosts or simply ethnographic sculptures that decorate this brilliant red room? Several small birds perch on the shoulders of the central figure, calling to mind St. Francis of Assisi and his sermon to the birds. The look on the protagonist's face insinuates something ominous, however. Perhaps the birds, believed in many cultures to be harbingers from another realm, portend disaster. The only furniture in the room is a table at the far right, which holds a chalice inscribed with a cross, a Christian symbol of the Last Supper. The lines that radiate from the cup similarly imply the presence of the Divine. The lamp above bears a striking resemblance to the one in *Guernica,* Picasso's devastating depiction of the consequences of war. Paladino frames his composition with scraps of lumber and uses molding that imparts a sense of timeworn history, of civilizations built and rebuilt on top of one another. Despite the vibrant hues and gestural brushwork, an eerie calm pervades the painting, suggesting that the tempest in this room is actually some sort of emotional turbulence or spiritual distress suffered by the isolated protagonist.

Carrie Przybilla

1. Quoted in *Mimmo Paladino* (Munich: Städtische Galerie im Lenbachhaus, 1985), pp. 43–44.

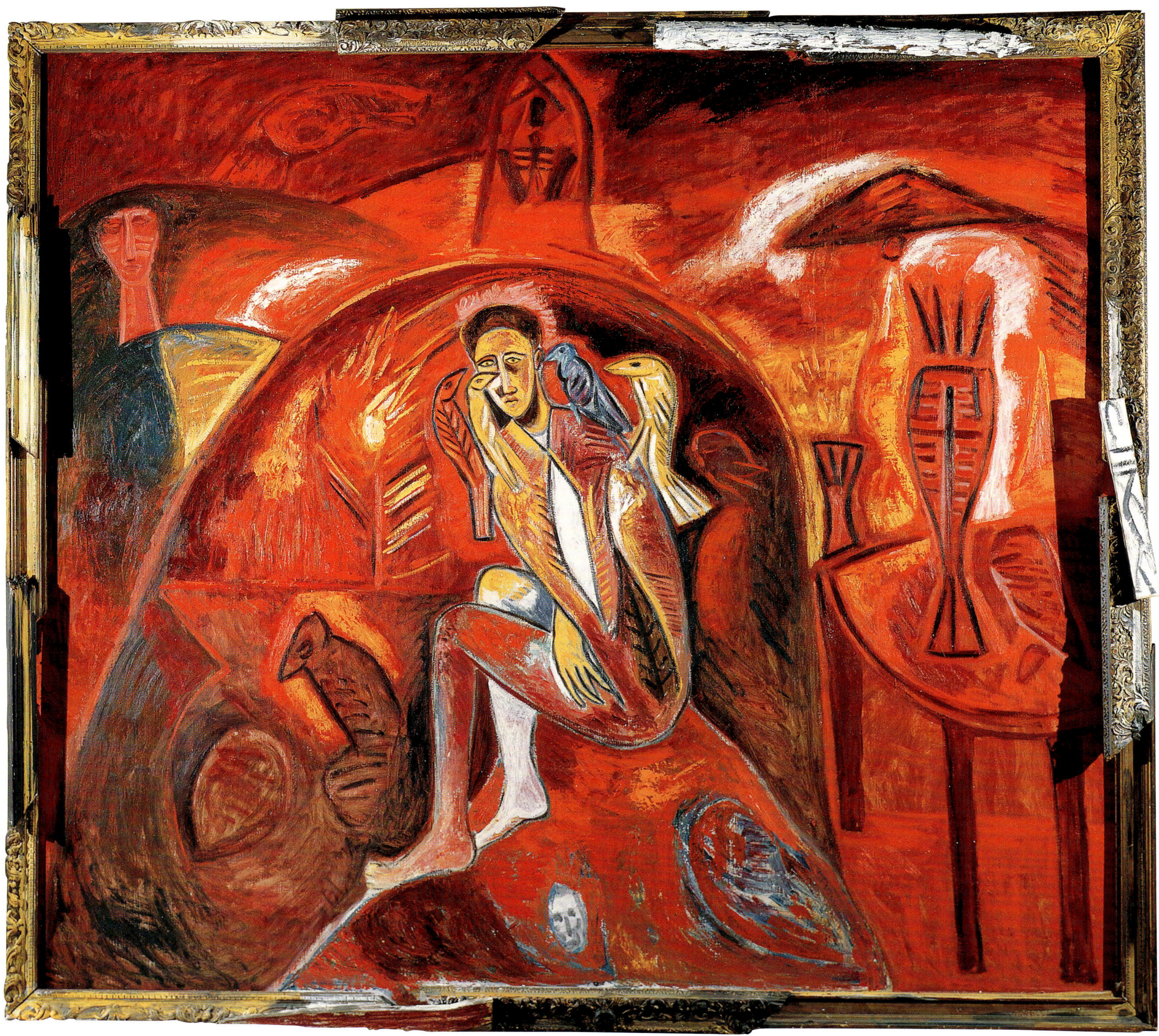

BETTY PARSONS

American, 1900–1982

Meridian, 1978

Oil on wood
37 × 22½ × 1½ inches
High Museum of Art, The Lenore and Burton Gold
  Collection of 20th-Century Art, 1992.50

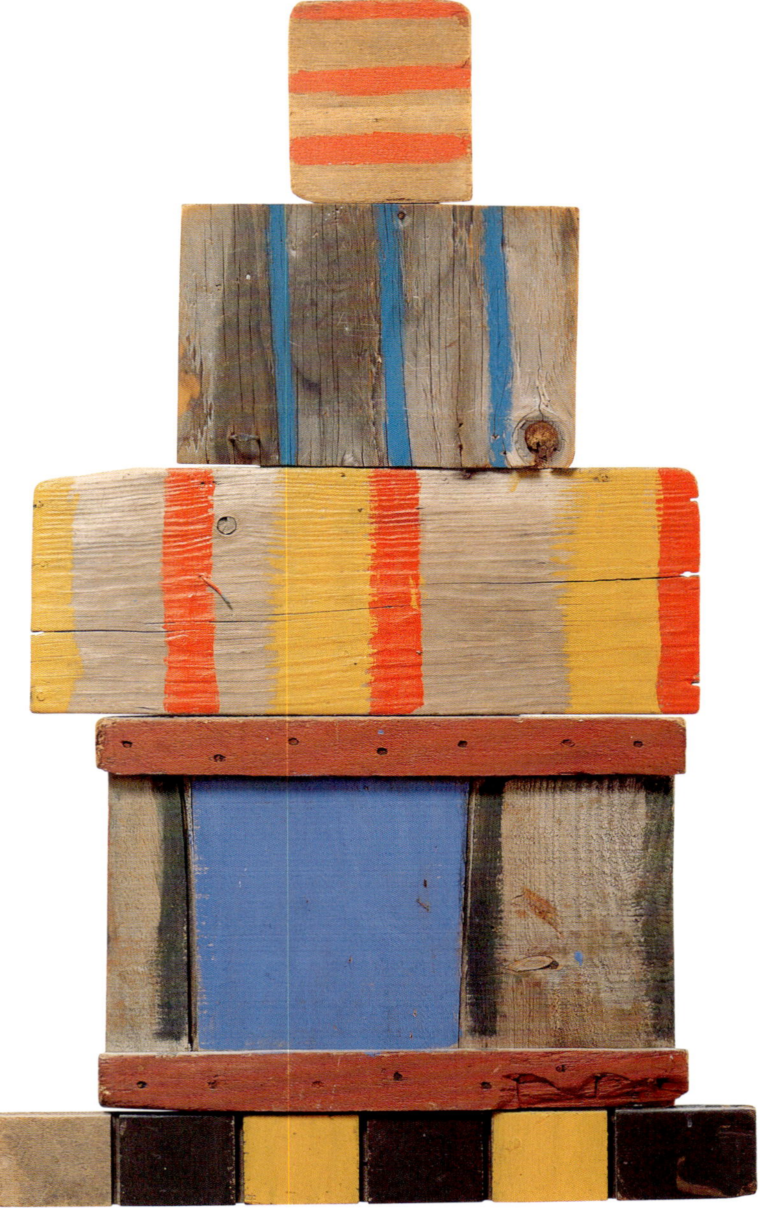

At the age of thirteen, Betty Parsons decided that she would be an artist after visiting the groundbreaking Armory Show. As an adult she considered herself an artist, though it was as an art dealer and a "discoverer" that she made her name. Through the Betty Parsons Gallery (1946–1982) in New York, she was a tenacious pioneer who showed work she believed in, launching the careers of many of the most significant artists of the twentieth century.

Upon graduating from Miss Chapin's School in 1915, Parsons announced that she wanted to attend college. Her parents insisted on finishing school. The daughter made a deal: she would attend finishing school *only* if she could take art classes. Parsons began her artistic studies in New York with Gutzon Borglum, who later carved Mount Rushmore.[1]

After a brief bout with marriage to Schuyler Parsons, she settled in Paris in 1923, studying sculpture with Antoine Bourdelle at the Académie de la Grande Chaumière, alongside Alberto Giacometti. Her mentors included Ossip Zadkine, Arthur Lindsey, Constantin Brancusi, and Alexander Calder.[2] Parsons's circle also included such American expatriates as Janet Flanner, Josephine Baker, Gertrude Stein, and Romaine Brooks. After the Depression had exhausted the fortunes of her family and former husband, Parsons was forced to return to New York in 1933. She spent several exuberant years filled with incessant parties and travels, residing for a time in California, where she studied with Alexander Archipenko.[3] In 1936, Parsons had her first New York exhibition at the Midtown Galleries. Soon after, she began working there.

Having finally discovered something that energized and sustained her, Parsons embarked on a career as an art dealer, working at the Wakefield Gallery and Mortimer Brandt Gallery before opening her own in 1946. She sought out artists who were propelled by some mysterious internal force and could express this inner vision. Not swayed by any current trend or established name, Parsons gravitated to works that were inherently primal, pure, and timeless. These elements were evident in "primitive" art (which Parsons periodically showed); she became a champion of contemporary art that opened up the human spirit. At a time when abstract art was just evolving, Parsons was able to recognize the energy, power, and integrity that lay behind the innovative work of Adolph Gottlieb, Hans Hofmann, Robert Motherwell, Barnett Newman, Jackson Pollock, Ad Reinhardt, Mark Rothko, and Clyfford Still. Her stable also included Joseph Cornell, Agnes Martin, Kenzo Okada, and (later) Ellsworth Kelly and Richard Tuttle. The Betty Parsons Gallery quickly established itself as the heart of the avant-garde, becoming a hub for artists, collectors, and critics of contemporary art.

Parsons also produced and exhibited her own art. Her first work was representational, but she shifted toward abstraction in the late 1940s. In 1959, she asked friend and artist Tony Smith to build her a house on Long Island, which served as her home and studio until her death in 1982. Perched on a cliff above a beach, this setting inspired Parsons and played a key role in her later work. Using pieces of weathered wood that she found along the shore, she made abstract constructions. *Meridian* is one such work. Produced in 1978, this assemblage consists of several pieces of well-seasoned wood. On each fragment Parsons painted geometric configurations in bright, contrasting acrylic colors. The artist saw these constructions as personages and felt that her role was to serve as a medium "through which perfection found shape."[4] Perhaps sensing mortality, Parsons aimed to endow each construction with new life and spirit. Certainly the title could refer to the zenith of her career as an artist. In the 1970s, Parsons had seven solo exhibitions of her work, and her output in this last full decade was prolific.

Trinkett Clark

1. See Lee Hall, *Betty Parsons: Artist, Dealer, Collector* (New York: Abrams, 1991), p. 24.
2. See Lawrence Alloway, "The Art of Betty Parsons," in *Betty Parsons: paintings, gouaches and sculpture, 1955–68* (London: Whitechapel Gallery, 1968), p. 10.
3. Ibid., p. 6.
4. Quoted in Hall, p. 164.

35

SUSAN ROTHENBERG

American, born 1945

Skating an Eight, 1983

Oil on canvas
63 × 41 inches
Promised gift of Burton Gold to the High Museum of
Art for The Lenore and Burton Gold Collection of
20th-Century Art

Susan Rothenberg played a key role in the resurgence of figurative painting during the 1970s, after a decade dominated by Minimalist sculpture. She first gained national attention in the mid-1970s with a body of work that depicts horses in profile. At first, she rendered the animals with a clarity and sense of order indebted to Minimalism but open to emotional interpretation. The artist has acknowledged that "the horse was a way of not doing people, yet it was a symbol of people, a self-portrait, really."[1] By the late 1970s, her work more directly conveyed feelings: she relied less on geometric structure and completely fractured the horse, often showing only a head or a fragment of the body. Although sometimes grouped with Neo-Expressionists like Jean-Michel Basquiat, Julian Schnabel, and Mimmo Paladino, Rothenberg concerns herself with the psychological state of her subjects rather than raw extroverted emotion. She is keenly involved with the act of painting and manages to invest every inch of her canvases with feeling without ever surrendering to expressionist abandon.

In 1981, Rothenberg began a series of works that depict the outdoors and outdoor activities, particularly those with repetitive movements. This shift in subject came at a turbulent point in the artist's life—she was about to move to a new home and studio, had recently quit drinking, and was preparing for a large exhibition. As she has dryly observed, "I don't think it was a time for contemplative images."[2] Although obviously reminiscent of her approach to the horse, this new work sought to "reinvent the body to express an emotional state."[3] The figure no longer serves as a passive object for artistic manipulations that reveal the artist's state of mind. Its own action within a given setting establishes the emotional tone.

Skating an Eight exemplifies Rothenberg's work from this period. To better express motion and fleeting sensations, she switched from acrylic to oil paint, which allows for freer gesture. She built her images with brushstrokes, rather than line, to convey the figure's physicality and movement. The skater seems almost to merge with the background in places, continuing the ambiguous interplay of figure and ground that has long characterized Rothenberg's work. The feathery brushwork creates a sense of flickering light that suggests an affinity with the paintings of Claude Monet. As in many of her works from this period, action is strongly associated with children's play, here figure skating. This innocent pastime takes on a sense of menace, however. The figure eight inscribed on the ice—a symbol of infinity—almost engulfs the skater. The large pine tree that dominates the foreground looms threateningly. The muted tones of the canvas suggest impending dusk and create an ominous, dream-like calm. We can almost hear the crunch of blade against ice and a hushed breeze through snow-laden boughs. Narrative—what came before and what comes next—seems unimportant, and appropriately so. "I don't mean to tell a story," Rothenberg says. "What I mean to do is catch a moment, the moment to exemplify an emotion. That intention is the same as it has always been."[4]

Carrie Przybilla

1. Quoted in Grace Glueck, "Susan Rothenberg: New Outlook for a Visionary Artist," *New York Times Magazine,* 22 July 1984, sec. 6, p. 20.
2. Quoted in Carter Ratcliff, "Artist's Dialogue: Susan Rothenberg," *Architectural Digest* 44, no. 12 (December 1987), p. 58.
3. Quoted in Lisbet Nilson, "Susan Rothenberg: Every Brushstroke Is a Surprise," *ARTnews* 83, no. 2 (February 1984), p. 53, as quoted in Eliza E. Rathbone, *Susan Rothenberg* (Washington, D.C.: The Phillips Collection, 1985), p. 13.
4. Quoted in Glueck, p. 22.

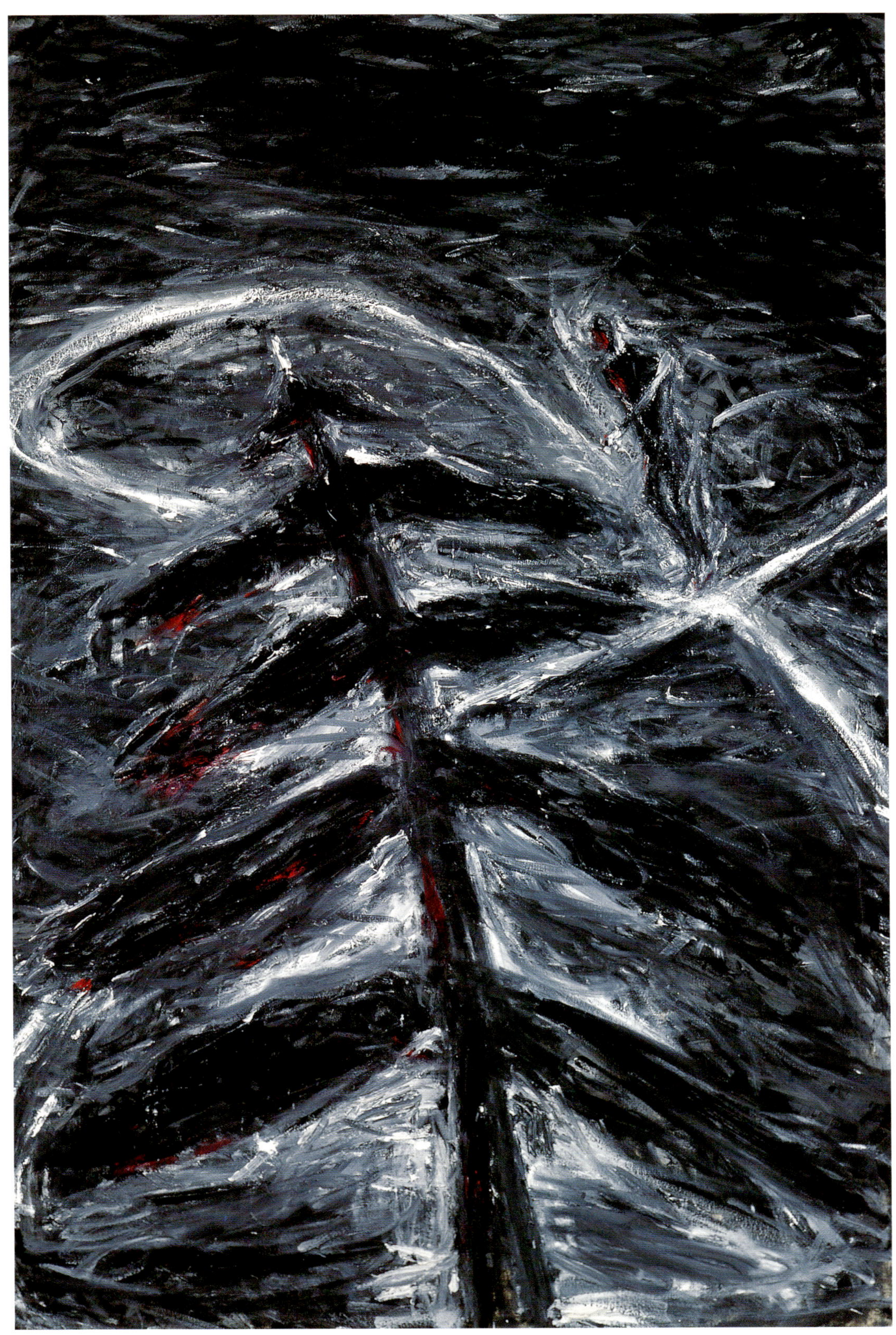

36

JULIAN SCHNABEL

American, born 1951

She Mistook Kindness for Weakness
(SMKFW), 1986

Oil and modeling paste on velvet
96 × 72 inches
High Museum of Art, The Lenore and Burton Gold
 Collection of 20th-Century Art, 1999.112

Julian Schnabel was propelled to fame in the early 1980s by his expressive paintings on surfaces encrusted with broken plates and other found materials. One of a group of New York–based artists who contributed to the international resurgence of representational painting in the late 1970s and 1980s, at the time he seemed radical as much for his unorthodox media as for his reliance on figuration. An artist of grand gestures, Schnabel generally chooses to work on a large scale. With equal measures of extravagance, intelligence, and bravura, he frequently sets aside traditional media in favor of sumptuous materials imbued with history. His imagery, always a delicate balance between abstraction and figuration, is laden with personal symbols and sometimes-obscure historical references that can seem disjointed if not impossible to decipher.

She Mistook Kindness for Weakness is from a series of paintings on velvet that Schnabel made during the 1980s. His use of black velvet evokes the dime-a-dozen tourist paintings sold in Mexican border towns like Brownsville, Texas, where the artist spent much of his childhood and adolescence. Although clearly thumbing his nose at traditional notions of good taste and high art, he employs the material without establishing an ironic stance. Rather, he embraces the distinctive properties of velvet as a support. The lush shimmer of the fabric gives oil paint a glow that Schnabel accentuates by using Day-Glo and metallic paints, underscoring his kitsch references. Velvet's light-absorbing capacity creates a sense of infinite depth that the artist repeatedly denies with thickly applied paint, which does not sink into the fabric and thus always calls attention to the flat surface. The caked paint on soft velvet creates an aura of sensuality and death.

Although the composition at first appears to be an abstract tangle of sinuous line and raw gesture, an overlay of at least two images—a stuffed rabbit carrying a club and wearing an admiral's hat, and a rocking horse—slowly emerges. Although they at first appear to make innocent reference to childhood, the frantic motion of these figures creates a mysterious turmoil that dissolves any sense of nostalgia or naïveté. The letters inscribed vertically along the right edge of this work, "SMKFW," are an abbreviation of the title, a typical Schnabel device that helps move the eye around the canvas while demanding closer scrutiny and calling attention to the cryptic title. The viewer can only speculate as to who "she" is and what the consequences of her mistake might be. Various connections to Schnabel's imagery present themselves, each vaguely menacing but ultimately elusive, compelling the viewer to look again.

Carrie Przybilla

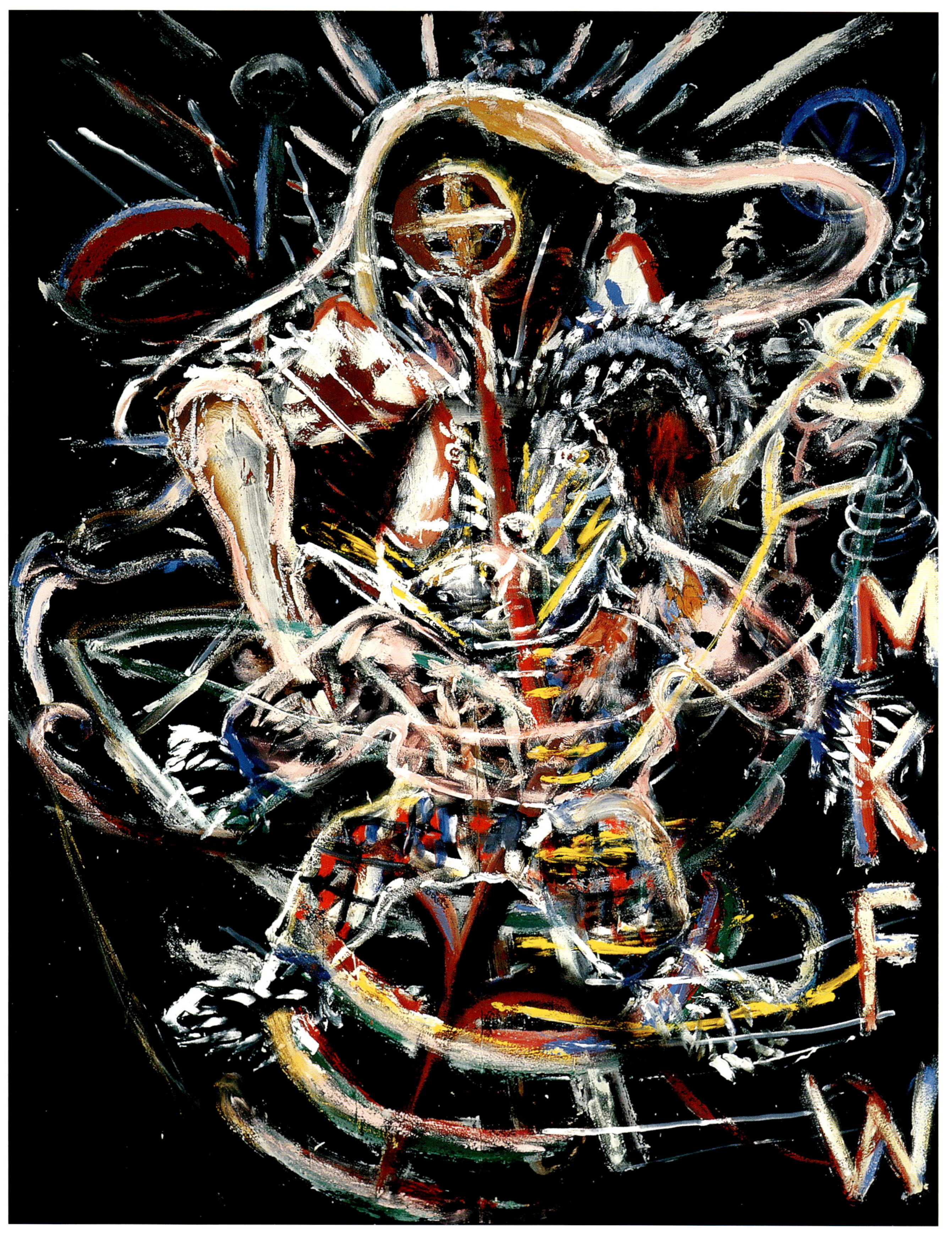

37

GEORGE SEGAL

American, 1924–2000

The Blue Door, 1975

Plaster and painted wood
47 × 20 × 15 inches
Collection of Pamela Gold Alexander

Although George Segal is best known for his haunting white figural sculptures, color always remained of interest to the artist, who began his career as a painter. Beginning in the mid-1960s, he frequently added color to his sculptures, often painting the figures vivid blue or flat black. He used both of these colors in *The Blue Door,* but only on the surrounding elements, where they accentuate the figure's lack of color, making her seem particularly fragile and vulnerable.

Despite their lifelike quality, it is hard to escape the realization that Segal's sculptures, cast from living people, mark the absence of a person more than his or her presence. The model is no longer there, but the space she once occupied is permanently fixed. Segal's sculptures have been compared to fossils and to the plaster casts made of the ancient victims of Pompeii, ordinary people going about their daily lives, who left their imprint for centuries in a mold of volcanic rock.

Segal's sculptures freeze people in moments of doing nothing in particular. They record fragments of lives, momentary details as if glimpsed in passing.[1] That quality is particularly evident in this sculpture, where the figure is seen only as a vertical sliver, a flash of white through a cracked door. Segal's sculptures have a mysterious quality, but this one is especially ambiguous: is the woman opening the door or closing it? Are we being invited in, or shut out? Is she emerging or retreating? Segal is noted for placing psychological distance between his art and the viewer, a separation made literal by the door in this work. He frequently incorporated doorways and windows as props in his work (his first cast sculpture, for which he was the model, includes a window), and such portals symbolize the boundaries between an intimate, personal space on the inside and a larger, public space on the outside.

Segal's figures are at once familiar and alien. Their real-life origins, lack of idealization, and the quotidian events they depict—their very ordinariness—strike a chord of recognition. Yet they are eerie, unsettling; they are clearly something separate from the real world. This is part of what gives Segal's art such raw emotional power.

Anna Bloomfield

1. See Paula Harper, "American Space," in *George Segal Sculpture* (Miami: Lowe Art Gallery, 1983), unpaginated.

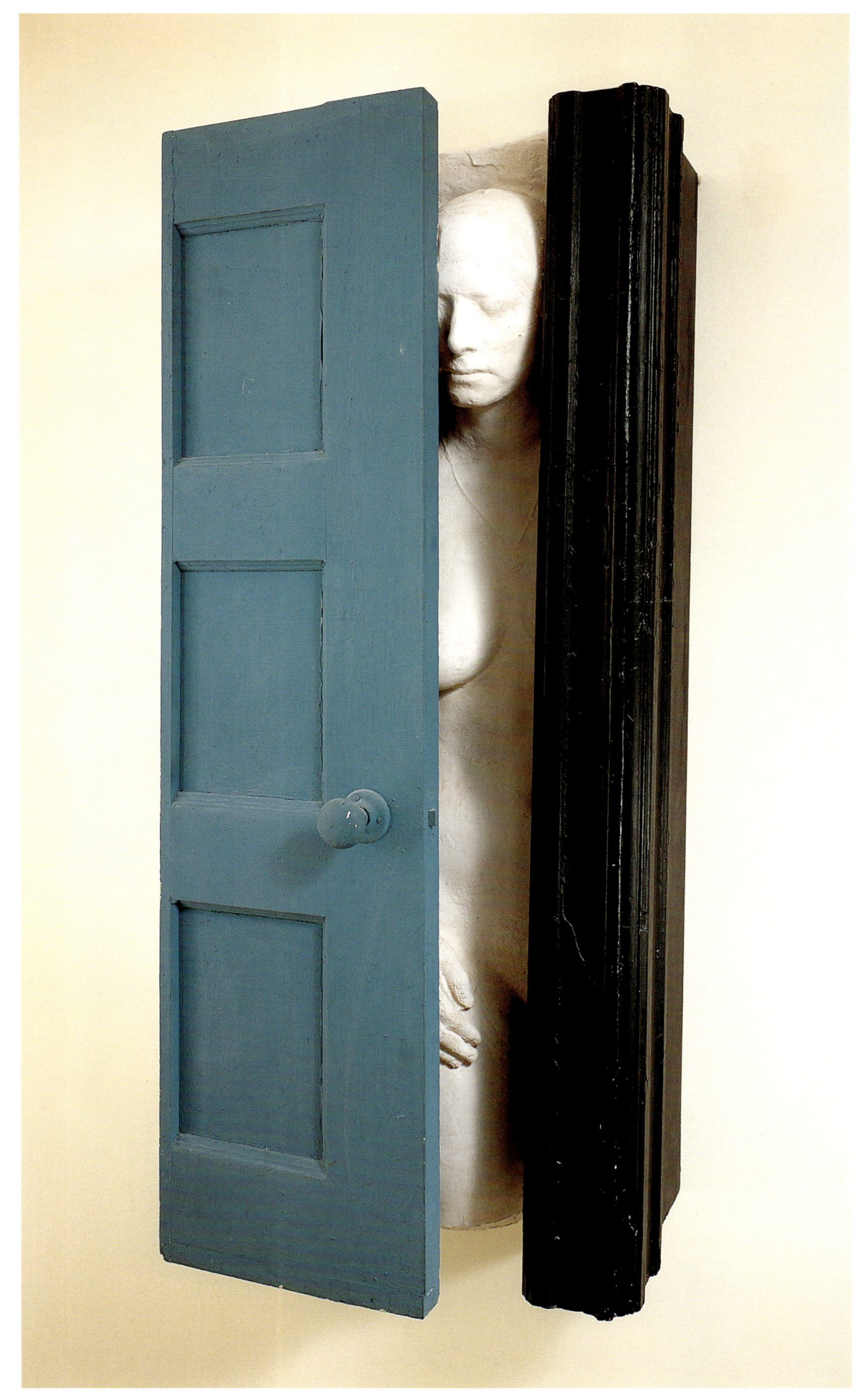

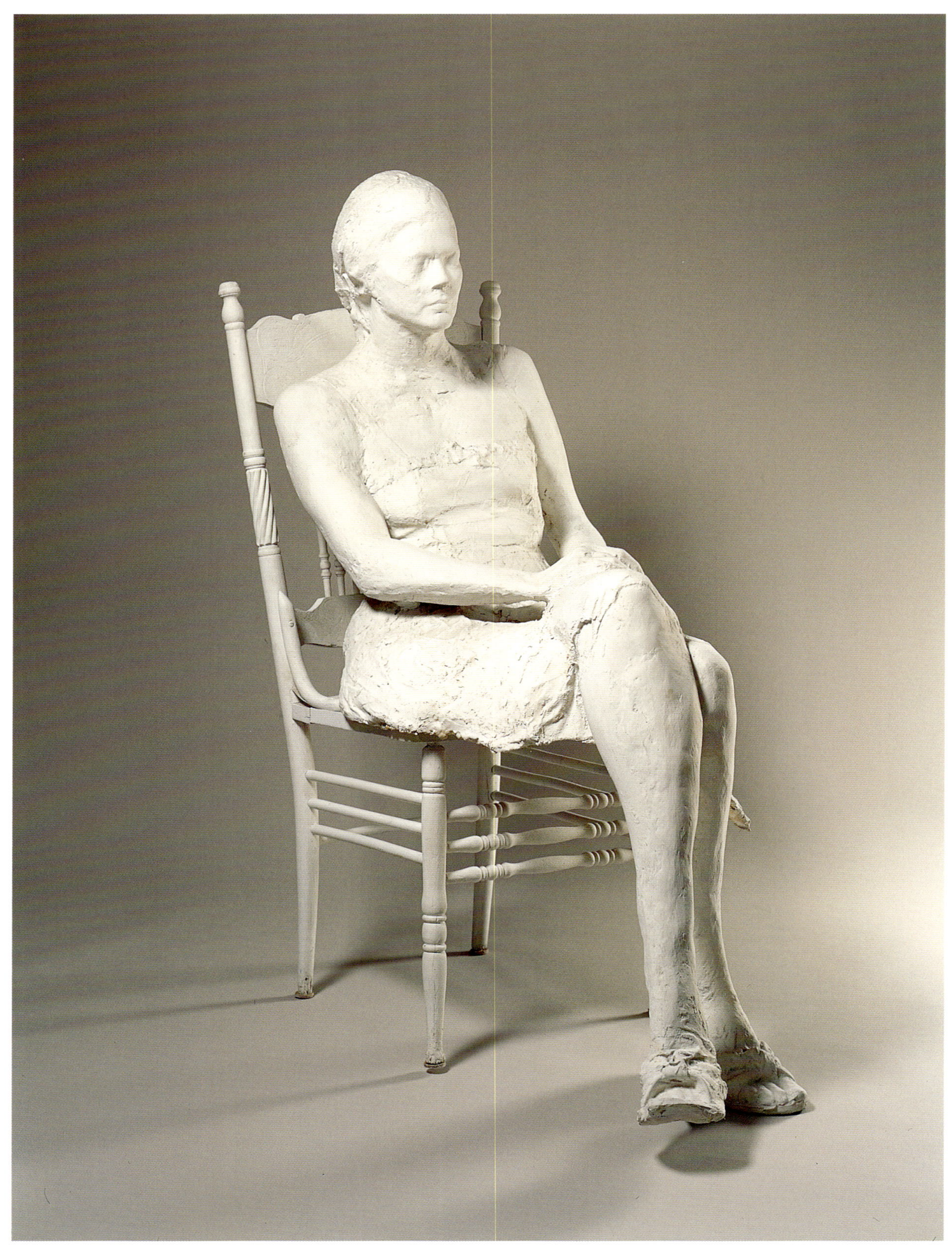

GEORGE SEGAL

American, 1924–2000

Seated Woman with Dangling Shoe, 1982

Plaster and wood
49 × 17 × 37½ inches
Promised gift of Burton Gold to the High Museum of
Art for The Lenore and Burton Gold Collection of
20th-Century Art

George Segal's sculptures, plaster casts taken from live models and installed within environments of everyday objects, are subdued, lumpen, ghostlike figures absorbed in solitary contemplation. Almost without exception they project fatigue, loneliness, withdrawal. Over forty years, Segal created a vast company of these "vital mummies," as Allan Kaprow once called them, and they depict, with great tenderness and sympathy, the alienation and isolation of modern humanity.

In the early 1960s, after a decade in which abstraction had dominated art, Segal, like many other artists, felt compelled to reincorporate recognizable imagery into his work. As he said, "I didn't want to sacrifice what I could see with my eyes, feel with my hands."[1] Because he looked to the everyday world for his subject matter and props, Segal has often been associated with Pop Art, yet while Pop was fascinated by commercial culture, Segal was more concerned with the human condition.

Segal stripped the elements in his sculptures down to a minimum. In *Seated Woman with Dangling Shoe,* the only details are the ordinary kitchen chair and the woman's clothing, a simple slip and pair of worn house shoes. The woman seems exhausted. With her forlorn bearing, she might have stepped out of a painting by Edward Hopper, an artist with whom Segal has often been compared. The work of both artists shares a sense of melancholy.

Segal, a chicken farmer before turning full time to art in the late 1950s, began making crude, life-size sculptures of people from the inexpensive materials he had on hand around the farm: chicken wire, burlap, and plaster. In 1961, he hit upon the idea of casting directly from live models by wrapping them, one section at a time, with plaster-soaked gauze bandages. After the plaster hardened—a forty-minute process that many of his models found agonizing—Segal cut the casts off and reassembled the fragments. In 1971, he changed his working method and began to use the shell as a mold, which he filled with plaster to create an impression with greater detail and closer resemblance to the models.

Yet these sculptures are far from portraits. Segal did not aim to capture the likeness of his sitters but rather something more universal through a telling posture or gesture. They are not realistic but retain the drips and irregularities of their making, which give them a rough, expressionistic effect. A disquieting feature of these sculptures is their lack of distinct eyes, protectively covered in the casting process. The result is that Segal's figures all seem to have their eyes closed, metaphorically looking inward rather than outward. If eyes are the windows to the soul, we can never know these people as individuals, and we aren't meant to. Segal's anonymous figures represent us all.

Anna Bloomfield

1. Segal, "Artist's Dialogue: A Conversation with George Segal," interview by Constance W. Glenn, *Architectural Digest* 40, no. 11 (November 1983), p. 66.

JOEL SHAPIRO

American, born 1941

Untitled, 1987

Bronze (edition 1/3)
48⅜ × 51 × 34¼ inches
Collection of Burton Gold

The figure remains an important source of inspiration for many contemporary artists, among them Joel Shapiro. Balancing abstraction and figuration, he pays homage to Pablo Picasso, Henri Matisse, Constantin Brancusi, and Alberto Giacometti, while striding toward his own identity as an artist. Shapiro's sculptures trigger an impulse in the memory as they invite the mind into another realm. Throughout his prolific career, his work has relied upon two themes: the house and the human figure. Shapiro's small-scale houses, first fabricated in the 1970s, transport one into a conceptual dimension. These simple, elegant dwellings are magical, enigmatic, and rife with domestic and personal associations. Guarded and remote, these Lilliputian structures inspire memories, emotions, and stories.

Shapiro's figures also command the viewer not just to look, but to take part in an active experience. The figure began to march across the artist's mind in the mid-1970s, first emerging in six etchings in 1975, before morphing into a painted bronze sculpture in 1976–1977.[1] Shapiro's figure has now multiplied, growing into a full-blown parade in three dimensions. Composed of simple rectangular blocks, Shapiro's figures are fabricated in wood. Some remain in wood as final works, but most are cast in bronze. Shapiro uses the sand-casting process, which involves making a mold of damp sand from the original form or from a plaster model. In this case each wooden element is cast and welded together. The texture

of the wood is retained, providing a technical history of the sculpure. Shapiro wants to duplicate the grain of the wood because "I have too much anxiety about the form's meaninglessness, so I want to have reference to the entire process of its making, from inception to conclusion."[2]

The elements are then welded together. At this point, it is important to Shapiro to try to maintain some of the spontaneity of the original maquette: "If you make a piece quickly enough, you'll find some posture that reflects your interior state. . . . You can lose a piece by the way you handle the bronze after you cast it. I tried to retain immediacy by keeping the record of the work's evolution evident. I retained the glue marks and the nails."[3]

Shapiro's frozen action figures explore motion and rhythm. His geometric personages are caught in time as they stride, run, tumble, dance, catapult, and collapse. The rich burnished surface of the bronze gives these works warmth and depth. Beyond investigating motion, balance, and gravity, Shapiro's figures have the capacity to spark memories through their dynamic attitudes. These figures are charged with emotion, suggesting joy or sorrow and sometimes even vulnerability or mortality. Ultimately, the artist wants the viewer to participate with his sculpture not only spatially, but intellectually.

The tension and kinetic energy emanating from this work invite many questions about the emotional and physical status of the figure. With

its ambiguous stance, it indicates a departure from Shapiro's more animated works. It could be a figure or simply an abstract construction. Even Shapiro is not sure: "I ripped the arms off and stuck them underneath the head, so it is sort of sitting there insistent. This piece was really about the elevation of mass, and trying to put this large chunk up off the ground at a precarious angle to accent its weight."[4] Like so many of Shapiro's sculptures, this work employs his characteristic vocabulary in a way that allows the viewer to make up the rest of the story.

Trinkett Clark

1. Hendel Teicher, *Joel Shapiro: Sculpture and Drawings* (New York: Abrams, 1998), pp. 92–93.

2. Shapiro, "An Interview with Joel Shapiro," interview by Peter Boswell, in Peter Boswell and Deborah Emont Scott, *Joel Shapiro: Outdoors* (Minneapolis: Walker Art Center, 1996), p. 30.

3. Ibid., pp. 28–29.

4. Quoted in Pamela Franks, ed., *Joel Shapiro: Sculpture in Clay, Plaster, Wood, Iron, and Bronze, 1971–1997* (Andover, Mass.: Addison Gallery of American Art, 1998), p. 89.

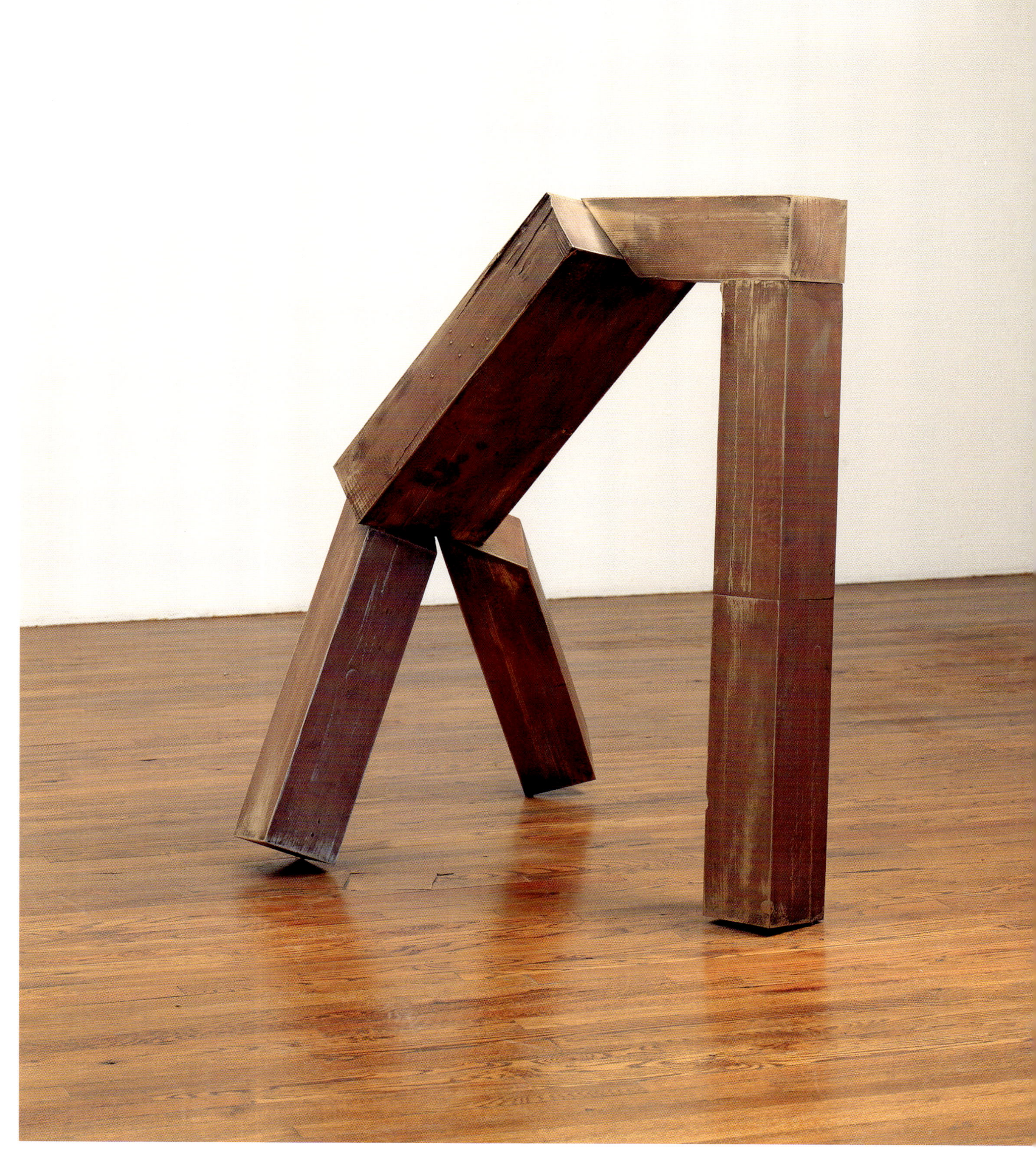

40

LORNA SIMPSON

American, born 1960

H.S., 1992
2 dye diffusion prints and engraved Plexiglas
  (edition 2/5)
49½ × 20½ inches
Collection of Joanne Gold

You no longer see black female characters in the media who are powerful even if they are sexually objectified. For instance, you once saw complex film characters like "Coffy," played by Pam Grier in 1973. She was a sex object, but she carried a weapon. That was more interesting to look at than the images you see now in a lot of music and movies.

—Lorna Simpson[1]

The photography-based work of Lorna
Simpson deals with concepts of power, self-image, and control. Using language as a primary vehicle, her approach involves the collaboration of simple image and text. It is a visual arts technique that dates back at least to Cubism and has been used with great effect by contemporary artists. For Simpson, the linkage of visual and verbal is a means of portraying the body as a weapon of defiance and a source of power.

Born in Brooklyn and trained at New York's School of Visual Arts and the University of California, San Diego, Simpson is best known for her series of life-size portraits of African American women wearing simple clothing accompanied by ambiguous texts. Her subjects are essentially anonymous: their faces are cropped out of the picture; their clothing reads as costumes or disguises; their gestures are clearly posed. As a result, the accompanying words direct the viewer's understanding of these stylized, ambiguous images. Although her roots are in the documentary photography tradition, by addressing cultural, political, social, and gender issues, Simpson moves away from literal implications.

Her work depicts subtly subversive body language that challenges stereotypes and expected behavior. In most cases, she presents her subjects as if they have turned their backs on the spectator/photographer in acts of defiance and control. When she portrays female characters in a frontal position, Simpson omits the face, calling into question the truthfulness of photography itself.

In *H.S.*, an unidentified African American woman holds a high school yearbook in a manner that suggests several possible interpretations. On the one hand, it seems to challenge the viewer to select a matching head for the headless body of the model. On the other, it appears to comment on the immediacy of racial distinction as an identifying tool, as few African Americans are depicted in the yearbook. At the same time, the idea of positive identification and the validity of the photograph are called into question, as it is unclear if the model is actually presented (in the yearbook) or merely a presenter (showing it). The unknown figure holds all the clues and thus is in a position of power. The sense of control is deepened by Simpson's discreet placement of the words "subjugation" and "indoctrination" across the image, giving the figure the function of labeler, as she directs the viewer to look, see, and read.

Amalia Amaki

1. Quoted in Deborah Willis, *Lorna Simpson* (San Francisco: Friends of Photography, 1992), p. 56.

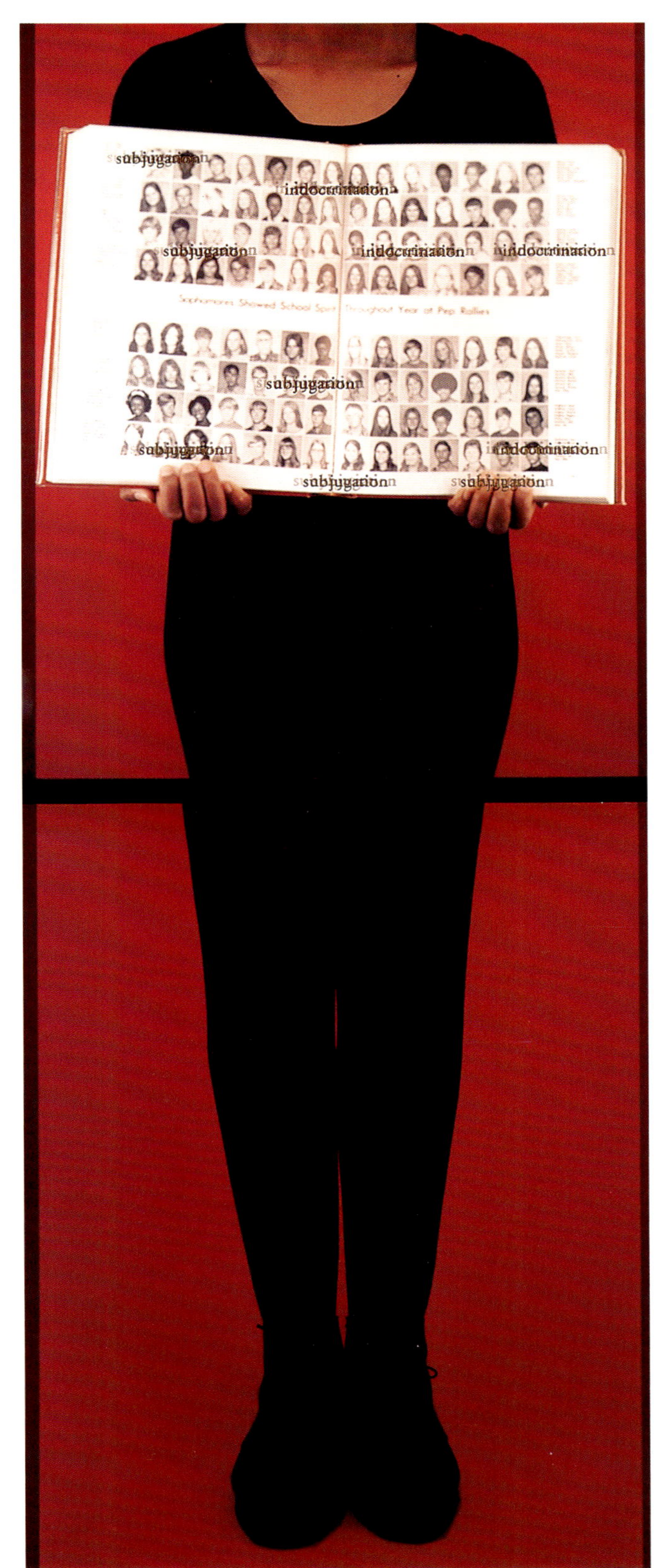

subjugation
indoctrination
subjugation
indoctrination
indoctrination
Sophomores Showed School Spirit Throughout Year at Pep Rallies
subjugation
subjugation
indoctrination
subjugation
subjugation

41

THOMAS STRUTH

German, born 1954

Museum of Modern Art I, New York, 1994
Chromogenic development print (edition 1/10)
70⅞ × 93¾ inches
Promised gift of Burton Gold to the High Museum of
Art for The Lenore and Burton Gold Collection of
20th-Century Art

Humorous and playful are unlikely terms to describe the work of Thomas Struth and his fellow contemporary German photographers, who in recent decades have established a detached, understated style in the tradition of the "New Objectivity" of August Sander and Albert Renger-Patzsch and Struth's teachers, Bernhard and Hilla Becher. However, this view of blurred gallery visitors in front of a sharply frozen Jackson Pollock action painting at The Museum of Modern Art is ironic to the point of almost being funny compared to his earlier somber black-and-white views of desolate urban scenes. Seen on its own, this work is almost a parody of earlier commentary on Abstract Expressionist painting. In Struth's photograph it is the non-objective painting that appears real, clear, and concrete, while the people seem unreal, vague, and insubstantial.

This photograph takes on special complexity when understood in light of other works from his *Museum Photographs* series, which depicts the interactions between people and the places where they see and experience art. Much of Struth's photography explores the act of looking, but the museum series he began in 1989 takes this theme to another level. The act of looking comes full circle as his subject of people looking at art (or often not looking at it) is repeated by us, the viewers, looking at his photograph. The fact that Struth made these imposing works almost 6 × 8 feet also creates a powerful similarity of space and scale between the people, art, and spaces depicted, and the viewer and museum display of Struth's photograph.

While his earlier urban views have an almost monotonous consistency in subjects and vantage point, Struth's *Museum Photographs* are varied in subject and approach. The photographs he made of the Seurat and Caillebotte paintings at The Art Institute of Chicago are viewed head-on, in a stark "neutral" museum environment like the Pollock at MoMA. Struth's images made in the Uffizi, the Louvre, and the Vatican, however, reflect the distinctive complexity of each interior and show visitors and art from a variety of perspectives. His view in the Pantheon, for example, depicts visitors dwarfed by the huge interior space. Grouping the art presentations of museums as diverse as MoMA, a classical temple, a medieval church, and a royal palace highlights numerous parallels between these institutions, their visitors, and the art. On one hand it suggests the role museums and art now play, transforming a Pollock painting into a kind of religious icon. On the other hand, as Guy Tosatto has observed, "These images of mass tourism subtly illustrate the paradoxes of a society which, in its desire to desacralize everything, has lost sight of the very notion of the sacred, leaving the crowds forever bereft of the deeper meanings of the works they come to see." Struth's photographs, says Tosatto, have "the feeling of witnessing a kind of modern pilgrimage in which the relics are not contemplated for themselves, but only in so far as they constitute the finality of a social ritual."[1]

Thomas W. Southall

1. Guy Tosatto, "The Time of Photography," in *Thomas Struth: Still* (Nîmes, France: Carre d'Art /Schirmer/Mosel, 1998), p. 14.

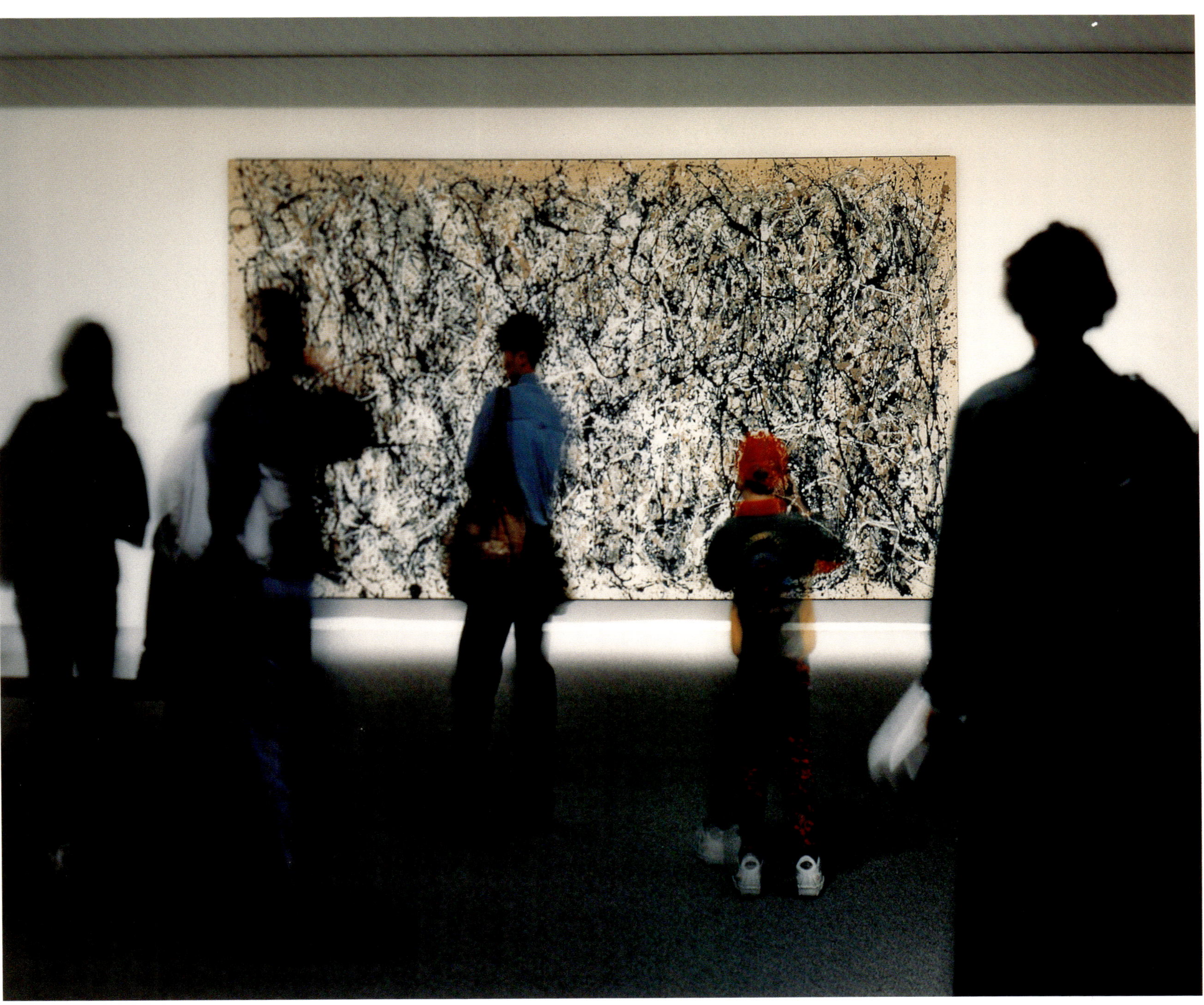

DONALD SULTAN

American, born 1951

Forest Fire, March 20, 1984, 1984

Latex and tar on vinyl tile over wood
96 × 48 × 4¼ inches
Promised gift of Burton Gold to the High Museum of
Art for The Lenore and Burton Gold Collection of
20th-Century Art

Ever since he was in his late twenties, Donald Sultan has been in the vanguard of artists who came of age in the late 1970s and early 1980s. Sultan has never been a member of any group—he resists any kind of labeling. He grew up in Asheville, North Carolina, at a time when abstract art was the prevailing trend in the United States. His father had wanted to pursue a career as a painter but instead went into his family's tire business. The younger Sultan attended the University of North Carolina, Chapel Hill, studying drama before discovering his true métier as an artist. In 1973 he went on to The School of the Art Institute of Chicago, where he was awarded his M.F.A. in 1975.

Sultan's choice of materials and imagery—and the manner in which he treats this imagery—has always distinguished him from his peers. He is known for monumental paintings that combine layers of industrial materials associated with everyday life, as well as seductively rendered charcoal drawings. Sultan's paintings emerge slowly from a time-consuming, laborious process: first there are four-foot-long wooden stretcher bars onto which a four-foot-square sheet of plywood is bolted.[1] Next comes a layer of Masonite, over which Sultan adheres squares of vinyl tiles to form a grid. Using this four-foot square as the standard unit, the artist then combines squares to make the actual composition. In the next step, Sultan applies several layers of tar—sometimes extending the tar over the edges of the support, sometimes leaving some of the tiles exposed. After the tar has dried (this may take up to two weeks), the artist has a matte black veneer on which to play. Employing knives and a blowtorch, he scores, gouges, burns, and manipulates his surface, outlining his image. Then he rebuilds the surface, using spackle, latex, and paint. The complexity of Sultan's arduous procedure contrasts with the simplicity of his subjects, and yet technique and image work harmoniously as a whole.

Sultan draws his subjects from popular culture, perhaps in homage to Pop Art. Through the years, he has looked to the industrial landscape (smokestacks, factories, battleships) or catastrophic events (fires, accidents, oil spills) for his subjects. He has also taken a more traditional route, using the still life as a vehicle of expression. In both his paintings and drawings, Sultan's images are cropped and isolated. They float in time and space, suspended before monochromatic grounds, thereby emanating a surreal and timeless quality.

In his "event" paintings, Sultan often uses an actual cataclysmic occurrence as inspiration, as in *Forest Fire, March 20, 1984.*[2] This vertical composition has a potent, sinister presence. The viewer stands just at the brink of the fire, facing the conflagration head on, the waves of heat almost palpable. The only color is the lemony yellow of the flames that radiate off of the surface, leaping playfully between the two dark silhouettes. These shroud-like forms are ambiguous. Are they pine trees or perhaps firefighters, slickers donned, anticipating the next burst of flame? Some of the edges of the work reveal streaks of paint amidst exposed linoleum. The resulting textures add to the smoky atmosphere of the painting. Discussing his "disaster" paintings, the artist has said, "I had no interest in narrative, illusionistic painting or being totally flat. I had no interest in being totally abstract, I had no interest in being figurative. I wanted to combine these things somehow to create a viable situation that both had power

and meaning and was riddled with kinds of paradoxes that feed on each other so they can have a
life."[3] Certainly the fusion of Sultan's subject with
his process creates a "unity of opposites."[4] *Forest
Fire* is simultaneously heavy and weightless, elo-
quent and mysterious, dramatic and contemplative, abstract and representational. It embraces
Donald Sultan's search for aesthetic freedom
while captivating the viewer with an eerie
beauty.

Trinkett Clark

1. Ian Dunlop and Lynne Warren, *Donald Sultan* (Chicago:
   Museum of Contemporary Art; New York: Abrams,
   1987), pp. 13–14.
2. Sultan includes the date of completion of each work in
   its title.
3. Sultan, *An Interview with Donald Sultan by Barbara
   Rose,* interview by Barbara Rose (New York: Random
   House, 1988), p. 36.
4. Donald B. Kuspit, "Donald Sultan at Blum Helman,"
   Art in America 72 (May 1984), p. 178.

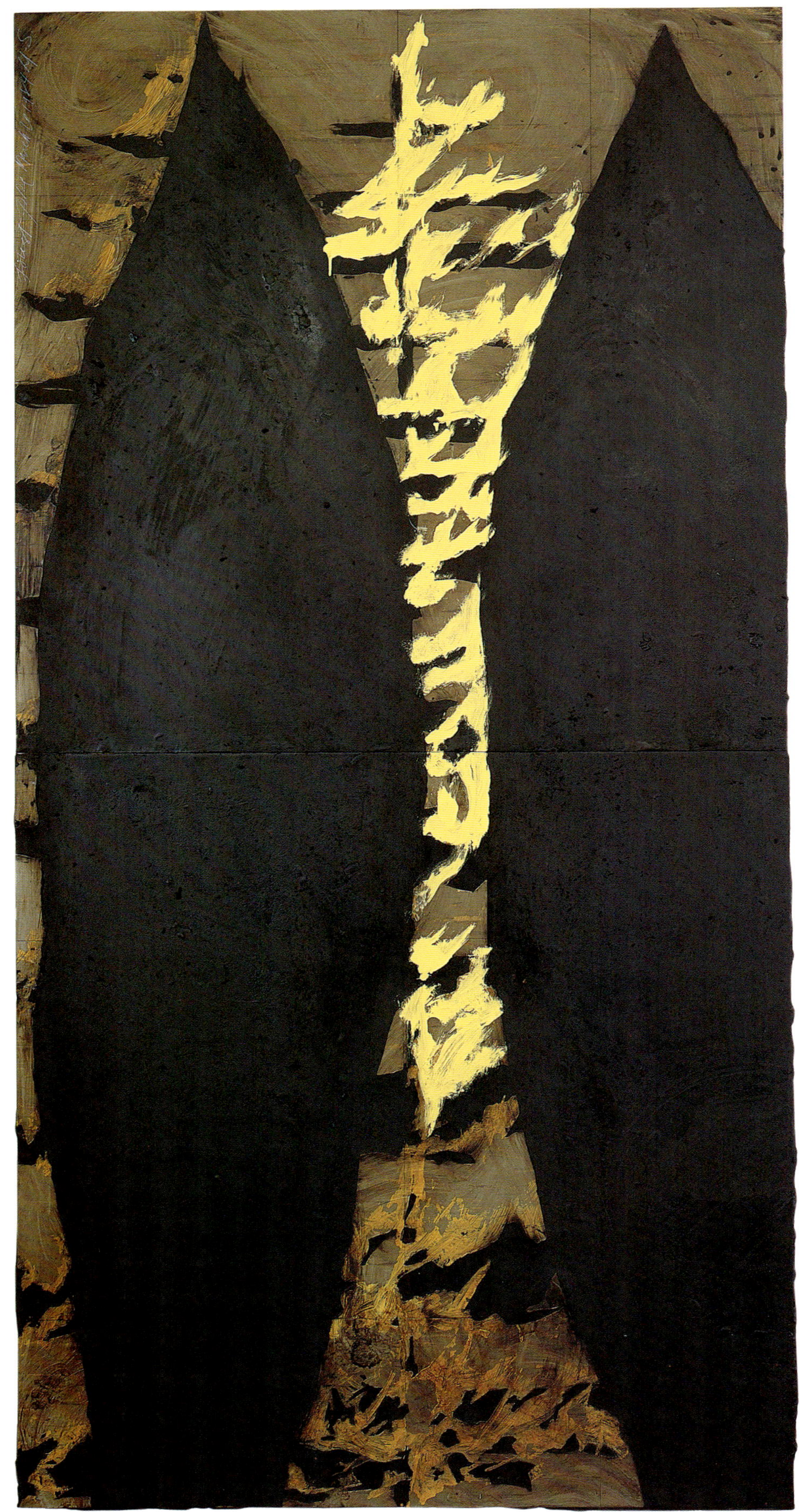

43

DONALD SULTAN

American, born 1951

Black Lemons and Eggs, May 18, 1987,
1987
Charcoal on paper
60 × 50 inches
Collection of Janice Gold Dietz

Always concentrating on several themes simultaneously, Donald Sultan has found the still life a mesmerizing subject: tulips, bugs, butterflies, pears, apples, and lemons grace both his paintings and works on paper. He explains this choice, saying:

> If I was going to be involved in abstraction and painting and figuration, still life was perfect because it could be very abstract and I could put a lot of things back into abstract paintings that had been removed, like space and volume and light. I could put in meaning and I could use black lemons and industrial things. I could work with scale and eroticism and sexuality and all of the things you find in life. The still life fascination came from the lemon.[1]

Indeed, Sultan's trademark is the lemon, an image that has been explored by artists for centuries. Attracted to its organic shape and sensuality, he has employed it in his vocabulary since 1983, after examining some of Édouard Manet's lemons in the exhibition *Manet: 1832–1883* at The Metropolitan Museum of Art in New York. Remembering this experience, he said, "I was through doing the tulips. I was with another artist, and he observed that a Manet lemon wasn't much different from the tulips. I thought 'He's right—the lemon is a tulip turned sideways.' Voilà! I did one little lemon still life—and I liked it so much! It's such an odd shape, it's so abstract and so real at the same time. Lemons are heavy, too. They have a lot of weight."[2]

Sultan depicts the fruit in groups—in his drawings, they are lushly rendered in charcoal and graphite on large sheets of paper. As demonstrated by *Black Lemons and Eggs,* Sultan transfers his proclivity for the lemon to the egg as well. Detached from reality, these giant forms hover sensuously in space. Their blurred, ambiguous edges intensify the brooding quality of the composition. An element of mystery pervades, reinforced by Sultan's vague title: is the image in the top right corner an egg or a lemon? What about the form on the bottom? We are compelled to ponder beyond balance and form. Ultimately, Sultan is guiding us, even imploring us to imagine beyond the simple image.

In the end, Sultan does not produce a traditional still life. What the artist is trying to achieve in his body of work is a reaction. Through his subject matter and the way he manipulates it, Sultan transforms the visual image into a more elusive impulse, generating hidden associations and memories lodged in the subconscious.

Trinkett Clark

1. Sultan, *An Interview with Donald Sultan by Barbara Rose,* interview by Barbara Rose (New York: Random House, 1988), pp. 77–78.
2. Quoted in Gerrit Henry, "Donald Sultan: His Prints," *The Print Collector's Newsletter* XVI, no. 6 (January–February 1986), p. 196.

44

ABRAHAM WALKOWITZ

American, born Russia, 1880–1965

Isadora Duncan

Ink and graphite on paper
13⅞ × 8⅜ inches
High Museum of Art, The Lenore and Burton Gold
   Collection of 20th-Century Art, 1981.55

Abraham Walkowitz has often been regarded as one of the pioneering spirits behind the modernist movement of American art in the early twentieth century. Born in western Siberia, Walkowitz immigrated with his family to the United States in 1889. After an arduous Atlantic crossing, the Walkowitz family settled in New York City's Lower East Side, where his mother operated a newsstand, and Abraham and his two surviving siblings attended public school. He also studied the violin and demonstrated an aptitude for drawing and painting, which he eventually pursued at the Cooper Union, the Educational Alliance (a community house on the east side), and the National Academy of Design.

From an early age, Walkowitz captured the pace of the city with its modern architecture, bustling street life, and crowds of people. He was particularly accomplished at portraying the working-class people he encountered every day in the Jewish ghetto, and these early portraits are perhaps his most haunting and compelling works. Between 1900 and 1906, Walkowitz taught art at the Educational Alliance, establishing himself as a painter, draftsman, and printmaker.

In 1906, Walkowitz traveled to England, Holland, and Italy before settling in Paris, where he was saturated in the vibrant art world. He visited museums and galleries and enrolled in the Académie Julien, where he became a close associate of the painter Max Weber. Weber introduced Walkowitz to his friends, including Henri Matisse, Pablo Picasso, and Auguste Rodin. Upon his return to New York in 1907, Walkowitz incorporated into his work what he had discovered, in particular the tenets of the Fauves, the Cubists, and the Futurists. Walkowitz straddled the representational and the abstract, the figurative and the gestural. Through Marsden Hartley, Walkowitz met the photographer Alfred Stieglitz and became a part of Stieglitz's circle, along with Hartley, John Marin, Arthur Dove, and Georgia O'Keeffe. Walkowitz was now a member of the American avant-garde. By 1912 he was exhibiting his work at Stieglitz's famous Gallery 291, and in 1913 he participated in the historic Armory Show. After Stieglitz closed his gallery in 1917, Walkowitz did not find as many opportunities to exhibit his work, and his career never regained the momentum of those years after Paris. Due to failing eyesight, he was unable to paint much after the mid-1940s, but he retained a kind of advisory role in the art world until his death in 1965.

Abraham Walkowitz returned repeatedly to his favorite subject. It was in Rodin's studio in 1906 that Walkowitz first encountered Isadora Duncan, one of the most illustrious figures of modern dance. Soon after they met, Walkowitz saw her dance and was forever enchanted with her expressive and interpretive performance.

Many years later he still was able to recall her:
"She was a Muse. She had no laws. She didn't
dance according to rules. She created. Her body
was music. It was a body electric, like Walt
Whitman."[1]

Drawing from memory, Walkowitz captured
Duncan in thousands of drawings over the next
thirty years. Whether executed in pen and ink or
watercolor, the drawings are characterized by
rhythmic lines and simple compositions. Without
articulating muscles or physical details, Walkowitz
was able to render Duncan's fluid movements
and inner force. In this drawing, Duncan is poised
in mid-stride with arm raised, her Greek-inspired
drapery delineated with just a few undulating
strokes of ink. This linear work is typical of the
spontaneous and minimal manner with which
Abraham Walkowitz was able to convey the
spirit, drama, and energy of his muse.

Trinkett Clark

1. Walkowitz, "A Tape Recorded Interview with Abraham
   Walkowitz," interview by Abram Lerner and Bartlett
   Cowdrey, *Journal of the Archives of American Art* 9
   (January 1969), p. 15, as cited in William Innes Homer,
   Alfred Stieglitz and the American Avant-Garde (Boston:
   New York Graphic Society, 1977), p. 140.

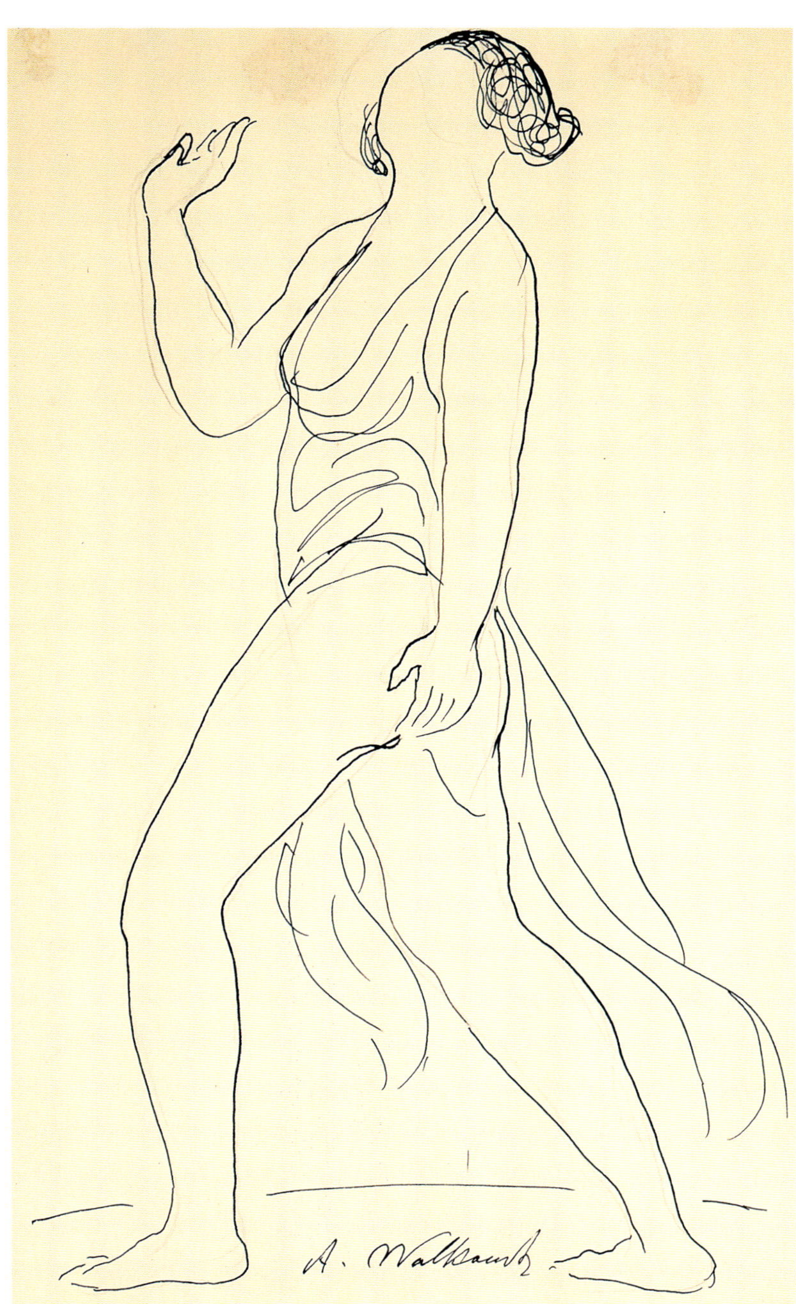

45

GARRY WINOGRAND

American, 1928–1984

Coney Island, New York, ca. 1960

Gelatin silver print
11 × 13⅞ inches
High Museum of Art, The Lenore and Burton Gold
Collection of 20th-Century Art, 1982.8

When Garry Winogrand's photography began drawing attention in the early 1960s, the description "snapshot-like" was perhaps too freely applied. Winogrand and many of his rebellious colleagues seemed so indifferent to established traditions of composition and technique that their detractors, according to John Szarkowski, labeled them the "quality be damned school."[1] *Coney Island, New York,* like much of Winogrand's work of the 1960s, has a casual, offhand quality that might seem almost amateurish on first viewing. The somewhat flat, low-contrast printing and grainy texture might have been an affront to viewers who expected sharp detail and a full range of tones. The composition is an even greater challenge to tradition because it awkwardly crops the figures at the bottom and right of the frame, and the head of the central standing figure is crudely blocked by a beam.

How were viewers supposed to read Winogrand's work? The mix of black and white beachgoers finding cool shelter in the shadows of the boardwalk might suggest social commentary at the dawn of a decade of civil rights struggles. What is the meaning of the headless man? Is the continuation of his figure by the metal pipe a comment on the mindless machine age, a surreal discovery like some Max Ernst collage? While there is visual irony in this photograph and throughout much of Winogrand's work, the artist strongly resisted any attempt to read a specific meaning and narrative into his images. The question "what are you trying to say in that photograph?" was dismissed by Winogrand with an offhand but direct response: "I have nothing to say. . . . I don't have anything to say in any picture. . . . I photograph to find out what something will look like photographed."[2]

Winogrand was thus rejecting not just the traditional craft of photography, but also the then-popular notion that photography, especially documentary photography and photojournalism, should have a narrative function and a purpose —to convince and persuade viewers. Instead, Winogrand was interested in simply discovering how the camera and film capture and transform the world. The challenge of photography for Winogrand was largely formal, and he was drawn to unconventional subjects and pictorial solutions because "you have more to contend with. . . . It makes the problem a bit more interesting."[3]

Although superficially similar to traditional photojournalism, Winogrand's photographic experimentation actually had a lot in common with Abstract Expressionist experiments with spontaneity and controlled accidents and Pop Art's deadpan approach to popular culture. Winogrand's testing of his control of his medium in ways that paralleled other, nonphotographic art of his time makes the Golds' inclusion of this work in a major collection of painting and other contemporary art even more interesting.

Thomas W. Southall

1. John Szarkowski, *Garry Winogrand: Figments from the Real World* (New York: Museum of Modern Art, 1988), p. 10.
2. Winogrand, "Monkeys Make the Problem More Difficult: A Collective Interview with Garry Winogrand (1972)," interview edited by Dennis Longwell, in *The Camera Viewed: Writings on Twentieth-Century Photography,* ed. Peninah R. Petruck (New York: E. P. Dutton, 1979), pp. 119, 127.
3. Ibid., p. 122.

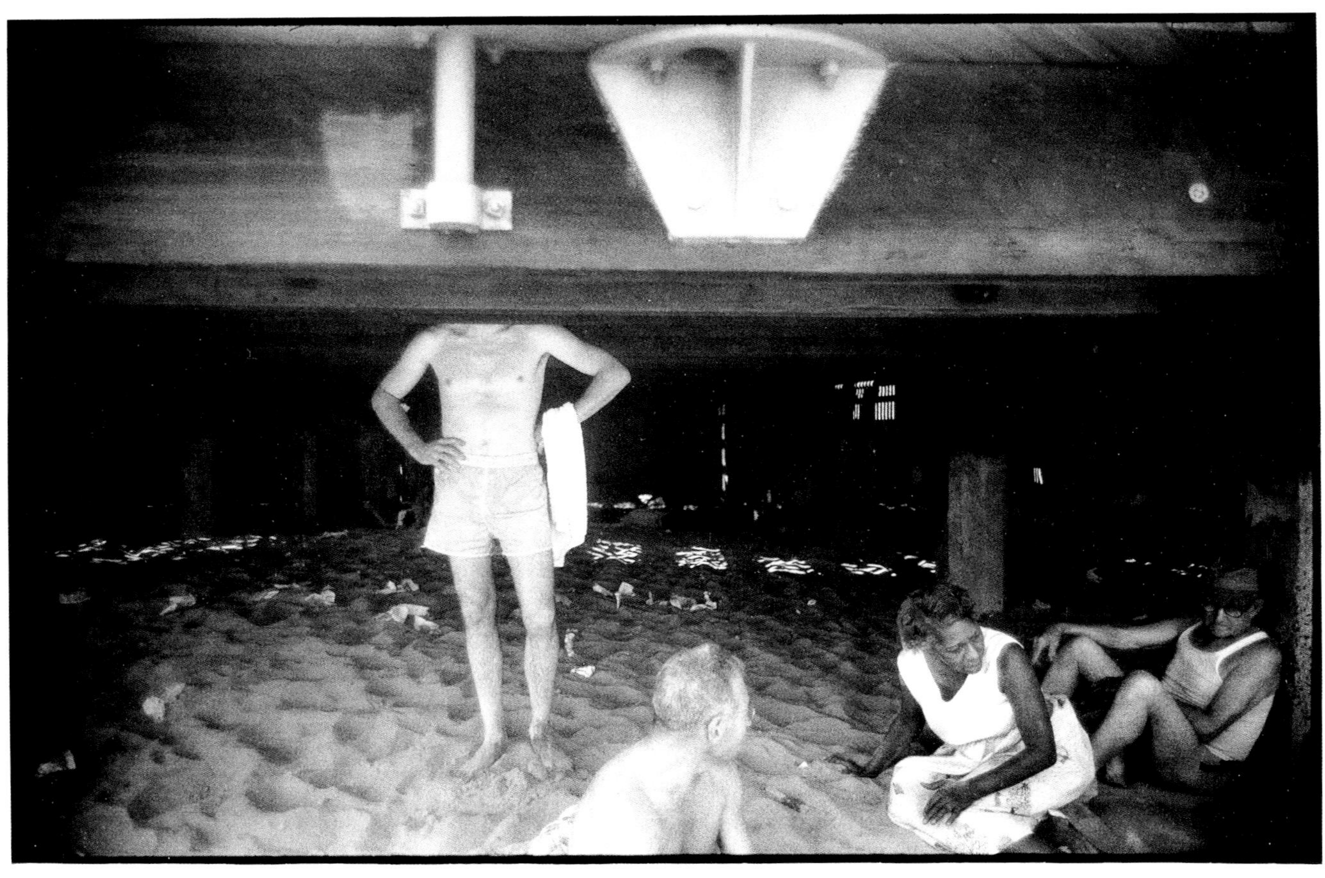

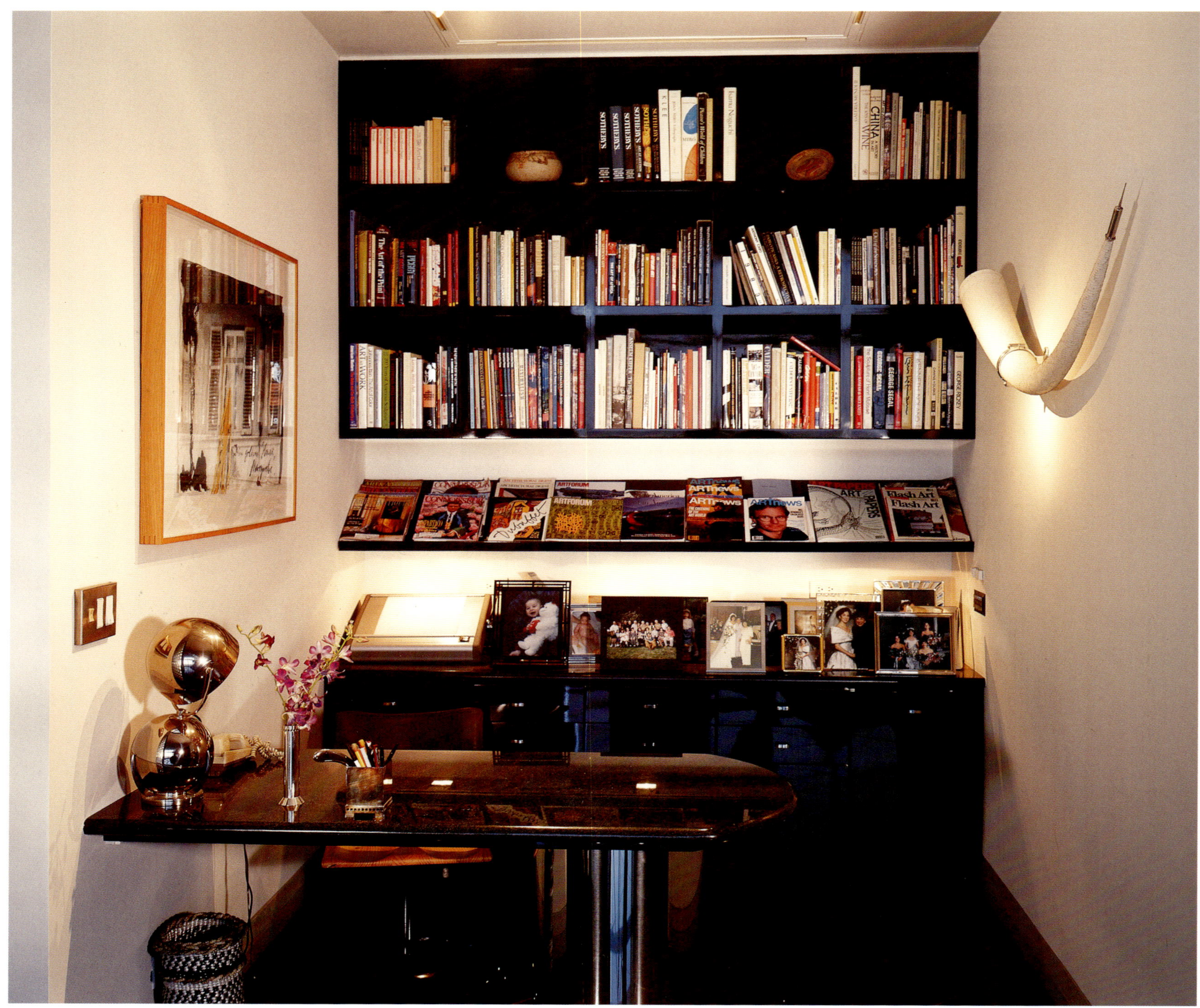

Lenore Gold's study, Park Place, ca. 1995

Ned Rifkin

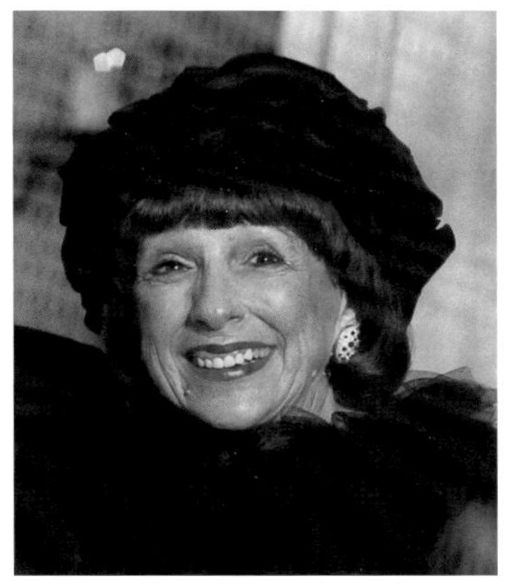

Leni was on a quest, propelled by her belief that if human beings continued to create fine, complex, and resonant works of art, then life must surely be a celebration, as well as the intricate and mysterious puzzle we can never truly solve. Hers was a search for the best of human nature, an aspiration for the noblest of human achievement.

Simply said, Lenore Gold was a rare individual whose passion for art was exceptional in fervor and intensity—a major force for the visual arts and culture in Atlanta. Her embrace of the most adventurous art compelled her into positions of leadership time and again, opportunities for Leni that were realized with impressive zeal and consistent intelligence. And her presence was not limited to Atlanta or to Georgia: she was a "major league player" in the world of national and international contemporary art. A few years ago, she and Burt were identified by a prominent art magazine as among the top one hundred collectors, not just of contemporary art, but of all art in the United States.

Her elegant home, an exquisite gallery designed and conceived by Lenore as a showcase for her art, dramatically testified that, for Leni, art was primary. She shone with profound love and pride in her collection. Her generous hospitality, the enormous pleasure she took in sharing her enthusiasm and insights about art, the sheer delight she radiated in and among her cherished paintings and sculptures—these are the ingredients of Lenore Gold's rich and enduring legacy to all of us.

Leni was a committed and valued member of the Board of Directors of the High Museum of Art—a leader among leaders—determined to make a difference at every moment, a steady voice and ferocious advocate for contemporary art, a persuasive and powerful fundraiser. Leni's rare gift was her immense capacity for envisioning what could be as well as an intense determination to get things done, effectively, with humor, wit, and, ultimately, with superb taste and just the right touch of style. Whoever met her knew, from the moment they saw her hat du jour, that Lenore Gold was an individual of dynamic creative energy and splendid strength.

Losing Lenore is nothing short of impossible to fathom for all of us in the world of arts and culture. The vastness of the void left behind by this unthinkable tragedy reaffirms the pivotal role she played in the vitality of our arts community. We must rededicate ourselves to celebrating Leni's spirit, maintaining the quest we shared with her and perpetuating the accomplishments of a most gifted and inspiring leader who taught us much about the will to continue to explore and discover the richness of the art and ideas of our own times. Lenore Gold was a star—her light is something that each of us knows, and each of us needs to keep aglow, even though the shining source has been suddenly and absurdly extinguished.

Lenore Gold died in an automobile accident on 13 February 1996. This eulogy was delivered by Ned Rifkin, then Director of the High Museum of Art, at her funeral at The Temple, Atlanta, Georgia, on 16 February 1996.

Amalia Amaki is an art historian, artist, and writer. Currently an Assistant Professor of Art History at Spelman College, she has written extensively on American art, particularly the work of photographer Prentice H. Polk. Her own photo-based works are represented in the collections of several museums.

Anna Bloomfield is a freelance editor and writer. She held positions at the High Museum of Art that included Assistant Curator of Photography and Associate Editor.

Trinkett Clark, an art historian and independent curator, is former Curator of Twentieth-Century Art at The Chrysler Museum of Art in Norfolk, Virginia, where she curated many exhibitions, including *Myth, Magic, and Mystery: One Hundred Years of American Children's Book Illustration.* Other publications include "The Drawings of David Smith" and "Land Ho! The Mythical World of Rodney Alan Greenblat."

Emily G. Hanna teaches African and African Diaspora Art History in the School of Art and Design at Georgia State University. She has curated exhibitions of African art at Spelman College and Georgia State University and serves as adjunct curator of African art at the High Museum of Art. She is writing a book that examines the historic and contemporary roles of African and African American artists in communities.

Peter Morrin was appointed Director of the J. B. Speed Art Museum, Louisville, Kentucky, in 1986. Prior to that he was Curator of 20th Century Art at the High Museum of Art and also served as Director of the Art Gallery and Assistant Professor in the Art Department at Vassar College. His many publications have addressed photography, nineteenth- and twentieth-century American art, modern European art, and the work of self-taught artists.

Carrie Przybilla is Curator of Modern and Contemporary Art at the High Museum of Art. Before coming to the High in 1988, she served as Visiting Curator at the Museum of Contemporary Art, Chicago, and as Curator of Art at Illinois State University. She has curated numerous exhibitions, including *Petah Coyne: black/white/black* and *Art at the Edge: Janine Antoni* and has contributed articles to a variety of catalogues and journals.

Thomas W. Southall was appointed Curator of Photography at the High Museum of Art in 1998. Formerly Professor of Art History and Curator of Photography at the Spencer Museum of Art at the University of Kansas and Curator of Photographs at the Amon Carter Museum in Fort Worth, Texas, he has organized numerous exhibitions with publications, including *Revealing Territory: Photographs of the Southwest by Mark Klett* (1992); *Walker Evans and William Christenberry: Of Time and Place* (1990); and *Diane Arbus: Magazine Work* (1984).